REGRESSION MODELS
WITH PYTHON
FOR BEGINNERS

**Theory and Applications of Linear Models and
Logistic Model with Python from Scratch**

AI PUBLISHING

How to contact us

If you have any feedback, please let us know by sending an email to contact@aispublishing.net.

This feedback is highly valued, and we look forward to hearing from you. It will be very helpful for us to improve the quality of our books.

To get the Python codes and materials used in this book, please click the link below:

https://www.aispublishing.net/book-regression-modeling

About the Publisher

At AI Publishing Company, we have established an international learning platform specifically for young students, beginners, small enterprises, startups, and managers who are new to data sciences and artificial intelligence.

Through our interactive, coherent, and practical books and courses, we help beginners learn skills that are crucial to developing AI and data science projects.

Our courses and books range from basic intro courses to language programming and data sciences to advanced courses for machine learning, deep learning, computer vision, big data, and much more, using programming languages like Python, R, and some data science and AI software.

AI Publishing's core focus is to enable our learners to create and try proactive solutions for digital problems by leveraging the power of AI and data sciences to the maximum extent.

Moreover, we offer specialized assistance in the form of our free online content and eBooks, providing up-to-date and useful insight into AI practices and data-science subjects, along with eliminating the doubts and misconceptions about AI and programming.

Our experts have cautiously developed our online courses and kept them concise, short, and comprehensive so that you can understand everything clearly and effectively and start practicing the applications right away.

We also offer consultancy and corporate training in AI and data sciences for enterprises so that their staff can navigate through the workflow efficiently.

With AI Publishing, you can always stay closer to the innovative world of AI and data sciences.

If you are also eager to learn the A to Z of AI and data sciences but have no clue where to start, AI Publishing is the finest place to go.

Please contact us by email at: contact@aispublishing.net.

AI Publishing is searching for author like you

If you're interested in becoming an author for AI Publishing, please contact us at authors@aispublishing.net.

We are working with developers and AI tech professionals, just like you, to help them share their insight with the global AI and Data Science lovers. You can share all subjects about hot topics in AI and Data Science.

Table of Contents

1

Preface

1.1. Book Approach

This book will give you the chance to have a fundamental understanding of regression analysis, which is needed for any data scientist or machine learning engineer. The book will achieve this by not only having an in-depth theoretical and analytical explanation of all concepts but also including dozens of hands-on, real-life projects that will help you understand the concepts better.

We will start by digging into Python programming as all the projects are developed using it, and it is currently the most used programming language in the world. We will also explore the most-famous libraries for data science such as Pandas, SciPy, Sklearn, and Statsmodel.

Then, we will start seeing how we can preprocess, prepare, and visualize the data, as these steps are crucial for any data science project and can take up to 80 percent of the project time. While we will focus more on the techniques normally used in regression analysis, we will also explain, in-details, all the techniques used in any data science project.

After that, we will know all about regression analysis in three modules, one for simple linear regression, one for multiple regression, and a final one for logistic regression. All three modules will contain many hands-on projects using real-world datasets.

1.2. Regression Analysis and Data Science

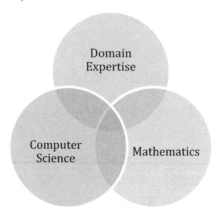

Data science is not a usual field like other traditional fields. Instead, it is a multi-disciplinary field, which means it combines different fields such as computer science, mathematics, and statistics. Because data science can be applied and used in different applications and fields, it requires domain expertise in this particular field. For example, if we use data science in medical analysis applications, then we will need an expert in medicine to help to define the system and interpret the result.

So, you might ask, what is the relation between data science and regression analysis?

Well, regression analysis is one of the fundamental concepts that any data scientist should know. It is a statistical method that can allow anyone to explore the relationship between any two or more variables. One of the variables is called *the dependent variable*, and the others are called *the independent variables*, or *the output* and *the features* in data science terminology. Also, regression analysis can be used for forecasting and prediction, as we will see throughout the book.

1.3. Who Is This Book For?

This book is for anyone interested in any application that depends on Artificial Intelligence and wants to know how it works, while he/she doesn't want to spend too much time understanding and studying the mathematics behind all this.

It is for anyone interested in getting to start working on real-world projects with real-world data. This book focuses more on explaining the concepts in simple language rather than going through complex mathematical equations. This doesn't mean that the mathematics will be completely ignored, but instead, it will be explained, also in simple terms, when necessary.

1.4. How to Use This Book

To get the utmost benefit from this book, you need to read every single part very carefully. So, try your best not to skip any part. Also, you will find that I refer to additional materials sometimes. You should make use of them as they will enhance your skills and understanding even more. You will know how to search for advanced topics after finishing this book.

Also, you will notice that there are a lot of hands-on projects in this book. Try to run them yourself and even try other approaches that you might find in the additional materials or that you think about.

1.5. **What is Regression and When to Use It?**

Regression is, as we said before, a statistical measurement used in finance, marketing, social sciences, and every other field. Its objective is to determine the strength of the relationship between one *dependent variable* which is usually written as *Y* and one or more *independent variables* which are usually written as *X*. While there are several types of regression analysis, such as simple linear regression and multiple linear regression, the objective is fairly the same.

If you are thinking about when you should use regression analysis, the answer is nearly always. That is because regression analysis offers great flexibility compared to other statistical methods, while also scaling well as you increase the size or the complexity of the problem.

You can use regression to control the independent variables which are needed when you want to minimize the effect of other variables on one specific dependent variable. Regression analysis accomplishes this by estimating the effect that changing one independent variable has on that specific dependent variable while excluding the other independent variables.

1.6. **Using Python for Regression Analysis**

Right through this book, we will be using Python as the programming language for all the exercises and projects. This is because, while there are a lot of software and other programming languages, such as SPSS and R, that you can use to perform regression analysis, they are either not free-to-use, very complicated, or do not have an active community like Python.

Python is a general-purpose programming language, which is super easy to learn and master, and very powerful at the same time. It offers a lot of ready-to-use libraries for regression analysis, with almost anything that you can think of.

1.7. About the Author

This book was developed by Ahmed Wael, who is pursuing his career in communication and information engineering, with a concentration in machine learning and big data. He is working in the field of AI, ranging from image processing and computer vision, deep learning and neural networks, natural language processing, data visualization, and many more. He is also a graduate of the Machine Learning Nano Degree at Udacity, where he is currently a mentor, tutoring over 100 students from around the world in the fundamentals of machine learning and deep learning.

.

An Important Note to Our Valued Readers:

Download the Color Images

Our print edition books are available only in black & white at present. However, the digital edition of our books is available in color PDF.

We request you to download the PDF file containing the color images of the screenshots/diagrams used in this book here:

https://www.aispublishing.net/book-regression-modeling

The typesetting and publishing costs for a color edition are prohibitive. These costs would push the final price of each book to $50, which would make the book less accessible for most beginners.

We are a small company, and we are negotiating with major publishers for a reduction in the publishing price. We are hopeful of a positive outcome sometime soon. In the meantime, we request you to help us with your wholehearted support, feedback, and review.

For the present, we have decided to print all of our books in black & white and provide access to the color version in PDF. This is a decision that would benefit the majority of our readers, as most of them are students. This would also allow beginners to afford our books.

Get in Touch With Us

Feedback from our readers is always welcome.

For general feedback please send us an Email at
contact@aipublishing.net
and mention the book title in the subject of your message.

Although we have taken great care to ensure 100 percent
accuracy of our content, mistakes do occur. If you
come across a mistake in this book, we would be grateful
if you report this to us as soon as you can.

If you are interested in becoming an AI Publishing author:
If there is any topic that you have expertise in
and you are keen on either writing or contributing to a book,
please send us an email at
author@aipublishing.net

2

Basics of Python for Data Science

This chapter will present you with a solid understanding of Python programming language in general, and more specifically, how to utilize it for data science applications. We will start by assuming that you do not know anything about Python programming. So we will explore all the basics together as this is a fundamental part of understanding regression concepts after that. After understanding all the basics of Python, we will introduce how Python can be used for regression analysis in terms of the tools and the libraries that Python offers, which enable us to perform powerful analysis in a few lines of code.

2.1. The Python Language

Python is currently the most popular programming language in the world, according to PYPL, with a share of 29.71 percent. It seems that this dominance will continue in the future also, as the trend is +4.1 percent, which indicates that more people, either programmers or people starting their programming career, will use Python in the future.

Python is a general-purpose, high-level, interpreted programming language that was developed by Guido Van Rossum back in 1991.

General-purpose means that it can be used for a wide spectrum of applications, such as data science, game development, web development, and many more.

High-level means that it is more humanly readable and generic for any computer architecture. This is opposed to the low-level programming languages, such as C and C++, which are more difficult for a human to interpret but much easier for the computer to do so. This makes executing the code much faster on a low-level programming language. Therefore, it's used more in very specific applications where the time of execution is a crucial metric to evaluate the performance of the program. However, if you do not care if the code took 0.0001s or 0.0002s to run, then a high-level programming language is the way to go.

Finally, Python is an interpreted language, which means that the code you execute is executed directly without compiling it first into machine language instructions. While, on the other hand, in compiled languages, such as C, the code is first converted into machine language and then gets executed. This makes the interpreted language slower to run than the compiled language. However, as we have just said, if you do not care about the fractions of seconds speedup that compiled and low-level languages offer, then you can start working with Python without hesitation.

Python has gone through many modifications and enhancements since it was first introduced nearly 28 years ago. Currently, there are two main stable versions of it, which are 2.7 and 3.6. In this book, we will be using 3.6 as it has more features and capability, and because Python 2.7 will be deprecated very soon, which means that there will be no support for it in the future.

Now, before we dive into the syntax of Python, we need to install it. We can do so using one of the following three methods:

1. Official Python Website: This is very easy to follow, but it will install Python only with no external libraries. Thus, **this method is not recommended**.

2. Miniconda: This will install Conda package manager along with Python. This method faces the same disadvantage as the first method, as all the external libraries must be installed manually.

3. Anaconda Distribution: This will install all the packages that you will need in many chapters of this eBook. Also, the installation of any additional packages is very easy and straightforward, and we will mention it when we need it. This is **the recommended method.**

Further Readings – Anaconda

For more details on how to use **Anaconda**, check this link: https://docs.conda.io/projects/conda/en/latest/index.html. Additionally, for quick reference, you could check the following cheat sheet https://docs.conda.io/projects/conda/en/4.6.0/_downloads/52a95608c49671267e40c689e0bc-00ca/conda-cheatsheet.pdf on their site.

Hands-on Time – Using Python in Anaconda

Throughout the following sections, keep Python Jupyter notebook open, and execute all the examples.

2.2. Python Syntax

Given that you installed Python successfully, let us start exploring it. We will start with the language syntax, which means the grammar of the rules of the language, just like any spoken language such as French or English. Also, like any spoken language, every programming language has its syntax, which can vary either a lot or very little.

We have five main rules in Python, which can be listed as follows:

1. **Line Structure:** This means that any Python code is divided into logical lines, and every line is ended by a token called *newline*. While you do not write this token yourself, as it is embedded in the language, it is very important to know that it exists, so you can understand how to write a syntax error-free code. This also means that a single logical line can be composed of one or more physical lines. Moreover, if a line has only comments or is just blank, it will be ignored by the interpreter.

2. **Comments:** They are very important in documentation as you will need this when you are working on a big project or want to share your code with someone else. To tell Python that this part is a comment, we use a hash character #.

3. **Joining lines:** This is usually needed when you are writing a long logical line of code, and we want it to be all visible on the screen. We can do so using the backslash character \.

4. **Multiple statements on a single line:** If you want to write two separate logical lines into one line, you can do so using the semicolon character.

5. **Indentation:** This is the most important rule, because, as your code gets more complex, you will need to define nested blocks of code. Thus, we will need a way to tell Python the flow of your nested blocks. In other languages, like Java or C++, curly brackets*{}* are used, while in Python, we use tabs to do the trick. All the statements within the same block should have the same indentation level.

2.3. Python Data Structures

Now, from here on, the book will be organized into two main parts for each section. The first part will be dedicated to explaining the concepts, while in the second part, we will focus on understanding how these concepts can be converted to Python code.

In this section, we will understand all Python data structures, both basic and advanced ones. To start with, we need to know that any code that we write is saved in the memory. To use a specific part of the code where we added two numbers, for example, we need to store the result with a name that both you and Python agree on, which is called *variable.* Of course, you can ignore that, but then you will need to know all the memory locations for all the results and the data in your code, which is impractical. Let us see an example.

In the following snippet of code, we are adding two numbers together. But where will the result be stored? In the memory, of course? But where? And how can we access this data again for any modification? It is extremely difficult to do so.

```
1+2
```

On the other hand, with a very slight modification, we can do the following.

```
x= 1+2
```

Now, the result is stored in a variable called *x*, which we can refer to from now on throughout our code.

Given that we now understand what is meant by a variable, let us talk about the basic data types. The first category of data types is **number**, which can take three different formats, which are **integer, float, and complex**. We will focus only on integer and float as complex variables are not used in regression analysis. In the following code snippet, it is clear how we can define these types.

```
x = 3
y = 3.5
print(type(x))
print(type(y))
```

From the code snippet, we can see that you can print the type of any variable using *type* built-in function.

Moreover, you can do any mathematical operation between numerical variables as follows.

```
x = 1
y = 2.5
z = x*y
print(type(z))
<class 'float'>
```

As you can see, the result is automatically saved as a float variable because we are multiplying an integer with a float.

Moving forward, let us discuss the second category of data types, which is a **string**. Strings are just sequences of character data, and we can use either double quotes or single ones to define a string variable as follows.

```
s = "Hello World! "
print(s)
print(type(s))
Hello World!
<class 'str'>
```

We can access specific elements of "Hello World" using indexing as follows:

```
new_s = s[2:5]
print(new_s)
llo
```

We can also concatenate different strings together.

```
newer_s = s + new_s
print(newer_s)
Hello World! llo
```

Moreover, we can multiply a string by a number. This will make the string get repeated several times equal to the number.

```
repeated_s = s*4
print(repeated_s)
Hello World! Hello World! Hello World! Hello World!
```

However, we cannot add a number to a string directly.

```
Add_s_sum = s+4
---------------------------------------------------------------
TypeError                         Traceback (most recent call last)
<ipython-input-8-c46ee2a4b7fb> in <module>----> 1 add_s_num =
s +4
TypeError: can only concatenate str (not "int") to str
```

To resolve this error, you need to convert the number first to a string, and then you can add them together.

```
add_s_sum = s + str(4)
print(add_s_num)
Hello World! 4
```

We can perform this operation, called typecasting, to any variable.

```
f_to_i = int(3.2)
i_to_f = float(3)
print(f_to_i)
print(type(f_to_i))
print(i_to_f)
print(type(i_to_f))
3
<class 'int'>
3.0
<class 'float'>
```

Now, let us move to the next data type, called **Boolean**. It is a data type that gets created to be used in comparisons and conditions because the only values in it are True and False.

```
is_true = 1.2 > 1
print(is_true)
print(type(is_true))
True
<class 'bool'>
```

Congratulations! You now know all about the basic data types in Python. Now, let us move to complex data types.

We will start with **lists**, which can be defined as a container of variables, of any type, stored together.

```
l = [1,2,5.1,'hi']
print(l)
print(type(l))
[1,2,5.1,'hi']
<class 'list'>
```

As you can see, to define a list, we use square brackets, and the indexing starts from zero. We can access any number of consecutive elements as follows.

```
new_list = l[0:2]
print(new_list)
[1, 2]
```

We can also use negative indexing to access the list from the end instead of from the start.

```
print(l[-1])
hi
```

Moreover, we can add or concatenate two lists together, and we can remove values from a list.

```
l_1 = [4,15,7]
l_2 = l_1 + l
print(l_2)
[4, 15, 7, 1, 4, 5.1, 'hi']
```

```
l_2.append(8)
print(l_2)
[4, 15, 7, 1, 4, 5.1, 'hi', 8]
```

```
l_2.remove(8)
print(l_2)
[4, 15, 7, 1, 4, 5.1, 'hi']
```

That is all you need to know about lists for now.

The second complex data type is called **Tuple**, which is a special case of the list where the elements cannot be changed.

As you have seen, lists can be altered, which means they are mutable, while on the other hand, tuples are immutable.

The following code snippets show that to define a tuple, you use the same syntax of the list but with a circular bracket instead of the square ones.

```
t = (1,2,5.1,'hi')
print(t)
print(type(t))
(1, 2, 5.1, 'hi')
<class 'tuple'>
```

However, to index value in a tuple, we use the same syntax of the list.

```
print(t[1])
2
```

Let us see what happens when we try to change the value of some index.

```
t[1] = 10
------------------------------------------------------------------
TypeError                         Traceback (most recent call last)
<ipython-input-8-c46ee2a4b7fb> in <module>----> 1 t[1] = 10
TypeError:'tuple' object does not support item assignment
```

For the next data type, we have **a Dictionary**, which is, just like its name, an address book, where you can find the address of anyone by just knowing his/her name. However, this name needs to be **unique**, as otherwise, you will not be entirely sure if this is the correct address or not. The person's name is called the **key**, while the address is called the **value**. The address is not unique, as many people can have the same address.

Take the heights as another example. Suppose we have John and Mary as we want to assign heights for them. Both can have the same heights, but the opposite is not true, as we cannot say that John is 180 cm and then say that he is 170 cm.

Moreover, if the height is the key, then we cannot assign the same height to different people.

To define a dictionary, we use curly brackets, and we use a colon to connect keys to values. Please also notice that, while tuples and lists are ordered, dictionaries are not ordered, and we use the keys to index the values.

```
dic = { "john" : 170 , " Mary" : 170}
print(dic)
print(type(dic))
{'john': 170, ' Mary': 170}
<class 'dict'>
```

Ok, so what happens when we assign two values to the same key?

```
dic_2 = {170 : "john", 170 : "Mary"}
print(dic_2)
{170: 'Mary'}
```

As you can see, the first value was overwritten by the second one.

Finally, let us talk about **sets**, which are complex data types that can only have unique value. Just like the dictionary, sets are defined by using curly brackets, do not have order, and cannot be indexed.

```
s = {1,20,4,5,6,1,2,3,4,5,3}
print(s)
print(type(s))
{1, 2, 3, 4, 5, 6, 20}
<class 'set'>
```

```
s[1]
-------------------------------------------------------------
--------------
TypeError                              Traceback (most
recent call last)
<ipython-input-8-c46ee2a4b7fb> in <module>----> 1 s[1]
TypeError:'set' object does not support indexing
```

That is all you need to know about Python data structure.

But the question is now, *When should you use what?* To answer this question, you can follow this list of use cases:

- **Lists:** The most generic data type. Use it when your data do not have any special cases, and you want to use indexing.

- **Tuples:** It is mainly used when you know that the data should not be no matter what.

- **Dictionaries:** Used when we want to have some sort of relation between some unique variables and other non-unique variables.

- **Sets:** Used when we know that any repeated data will be redundant.

Further Readings
For more information about Python data structures, you can go here: https://www.tutorialspoint.com/python/python_variable_types.htm

2.4. Jupyter Notebook

Now, let us explore the tools and the libraries that Python has regarding data science.

The first one of them is the Jupyter notebook, which is one of the fundamental tools that any data scientist uses right now. It is a web application that you can utilize to create and share documents containing code, text, equations, and visualizations.

If you installed Python using the third method from earlier on in this chapter, you should have already installed it.

When you open the application, you will see this User Interface.

From here, you can go anywhere, create notebooks, upload files, and much more.

To start, you click on **New** from the right corner. You will then see a new notebook created which looks like this.

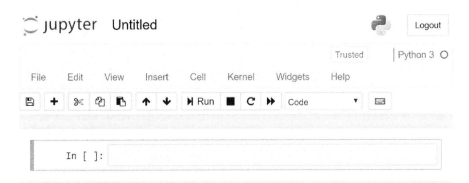

The most important part here is that you can either write in a code cell or a markdown cell. The markdown cell is to beautify and make the code more documented and clearer, but it is ignored by the Python interpreter.

Do not worry about all the other tabs, for now, as we will be using Jupyter notebooks heavily in all our exercises.

2.5. Numerical Python (NumPy)

NumPy is short for Numerical Python, which is a library comprising multidimensional array objects and a selection of routines for processing those arrays. Its main use is for mathematical and logical operations on arrays.

NumPy is also installed with Anaconda distribution.

To understand and practice the capabilities of NumPy, let us start writing some code using it.

We can import NumPy using "import", and we usually use a short name for our libraries as we will be calling them too many times.

```
import numpy as np
```

Create an array using NumPy by doing the following.

```
a=np.array([1,2,3])
print(a)
print(type(a))
[1 2 3]
<class 'numpy.ndarray'>
```

Now, let us see how to get the shape of an array. This is crucial in data science, as we are always working with arrays and matrices.

```
a.shape
(3,)
```

Let us create multi-dimensional array:

```
a_2d=np.array([[1,2,3],[4,5,6]])
print(a_2d)
print(type(a_2d))
print(a_2d.shape)
[[1 2 3]
 [4 5 6]]
<class 'numpy.ndarray'>
(2, 3)
```

Finally, let us see how to perform the basic operations using NumPy.

```
a1=np.array([1,2,3])
a2=np.array([4,5,6])
print(a1+a2)
print(a1-a2)
print(a1*a2)
print(a1/a2)
print(np.sqrt(a1))
print(np.mean(a1))
print(np.median(a1))
print(np.max(a1))
print(np.min(a1))
[5 7 9]
[-3 -3 -3]
[ 4 10 18]
[0.25 0.4  0.5 ]
[1.         1.41421356 1.73205081]
2.0
2.0
3
1
```

> **Further Readings**
>
> For more information about NumPy, you can go here:
> https://www.numpy.org/devdocs/user/quickstart.html

2.6. Pandas

Pandas is another critical library in data science. It provides high-performance data manipulation and analysis tools with its powerful data structures.

The main unit of Pandas is the DataFrame, which is like an excel sheet with dozens of built-in functions for any data preprocessing or manipulation needed. There is also a data type called **Series** and another one called **Panel.** Every one of them will be explained when needed.

With Pandas, dealing with missing data or outliers can be very easy. Not only that but also manipulating complete columns or rows of data can be easy as well.

Pandas also supports reading and writing different file types.

Let us look at the fundamentals of Pandas. Again, you must execute the following code snippets yourself to understand better.

We start by importing Pandas.

```
import pandas as pd
```

The following table summarizes the different Pandas data structures:

Data Structure	Dimensions	Description
Series	1	1D labeled homogeneous array, size-mutable.
Data Frames	2	and General 2D labeled, size-mutable tabular structure with potentially heterogeneously
Panel	3	General 3D labeled, size-mutable array

Series is a one-dimensional array-like structure with homogeneous data, while the size is immutable. Also, the values of the data are mutable.

```
pd.Series([1,2,3])
0    1
1    2
2    3
dtype: int64
```

DataFrame is a two-dimensional array with heterogeneous data, mutable size, and mutable size.

```
pd.DataFrame(data= {'col1': [1, 2], 'col2': [3, 4]})
      col1    col2
0     1       3
1     2       4
```

Pandas Panels are not used widely. Thus, we will focus only on Series and Data Frames.

However, you can use Panels when your data are 3D.

Pandas also has many data reading functions such as:

- read_csv()
- read_excel()
- read_json()
- read_html()
- read_sql()

Let us now work with a real-world dataset.

The first step is to change the directory to the one containing the dataset. This can be done using the os library.

```
import os
os.chdir('D:')
os.getcwd()
'D:\\'
```

Let us now use the different reading function that we have just mentioned. Pandas has a function called *head* that enables us to view the first few elements of a specific DataFrame.

```
iris_df=pd.read_csv('iris.csv')
iris_df.head()
```

	sepal_length	sepal_width	petal_length	petal_width	species
0	5.1	3.5	1.4	0.2	setosa
1	4.9	3.0	1.4	0.2	setosa
2	4.7	3.2	1.3	0.2	setosa
3	4.6	3.1	1.5	0.2	setosa
4	5.0	3.6	1.4	0.2	setosa

```
cars_df=pd.read_excel('cars.xls')
cars_df.head()
```

	Model	MPG	Cylinders	Displacement	Horsepower	Weight	Acceleration	Year	Origin
0	chevroletchevellemalibu	18.0	8	307.0	130	3504	12.0	70	US
1	buick skylark 320	15.0	8	350.0	165	3693	11.5	70	US
2	plymouth satellite	18.0	8	318.0	150	3436	11.0	70	US
3	amc rebel sst	16.0	8	304.0	150	3433	12.0	70	US
4	ford torino	17.0	8	302.0	140	3449	10.5	70	US

```
titanic_df=pd.read_json('titanic.json')
titanic_df.head()
```

	datasetid	fields	record_timestamp	recordid
0	titanic-passengers	{'fare': 7.3125, 'name': 'Olsen, Mr. Ole Marti...	2016-09-21T01:34:51+03:00	398286223e6c4c16377d2b81d5335ac6dcc2cafb
1	titanic-passengers	{'fare': 15.75, 'name': 'Watt, Mrs. James (Eli...	2016-09-21T01:34:51+03:00	a6e68dbc16c3cf161e3d250650203e2c06161474
2	titanic-passengers	{'fare': 7.775, 'name': 'Bengtsson, Mr. John V...	2016-09-21T01:34:51+03:00	50cc1cb165b05151593164cdbc3815c1c3cccb55
3	titanic-passengers	{'fare': 10.5, 'name': 'Mellors, Mr. William J...	2016-09-21T01:34:51+03:00	1b3c80a0f49d7a4b050f023381aec7ce40fe4768
4	titanic-passengers	{'fare': 14.4542, 'name': 'Zabour, Miss. Thami...	2016-09-21T01:34:51+03:00	30c3695bc6b529abe6fb6052648f9238371a189b

Now, let us work with the cars dataset and see how to select a column from it.

```
cars_df['MPG']
0    18.0
1    15.0
2    18.0
3    16.0
```

We can also choose a specific value in a specific column and row.

```
cars_df.iloc[19,1]
26.0
```

Moreover, we can choose the values that satisfy the condition.

```
cars_df.loc[cars_df.MPG>20,]
```

	Model	MPG	Cylinders	Displacement	Horsepower	Weight	Acceleration	Year	Origin
14	toyota corona mark ii	24.0	4	113.0	95	2372	15.0	70	Japan
15	plymouth duster	22.0	6	198.0	95	2833	15.5	70	US
17	ford maverick	21.0	6	200.0	85	2587	16.0	70	US
18	datsun pl510	27.0	4	97.0	88	2130	14.5	70	Japan
19	volkswagen 1131 deluxe sedan	26.0	4	97.0	46	1835	20.5	70	Europe
20	peugeot 504	25.0	4	110.0	87	2672	17.5	70	Europe
21	audi 100 ls	24.0	4	107.0	90	2430	14.5	70	Europe
22	saab 99e	25.0	4	104.0	95	2375	17.5	70	Europe

This can be done even with multiple conditions.

```
cars_df.loc[(cars_df.MPG>35)&(cars_df.Origin=='US'),]
```

	Model	MPG	Cylinders	Displacement	Horsepower	Weight	Acceleration	Year	Origin
243	ford fiesta	36.1	4	98.0	66	1800	14.4	78	US
293	dodge colt hatchback custom	35.7	4	98.0	80	1915	14.4	79	US
340	plymouth champ	39.0	4	86.0	64	1875	16.4	81	US
372	plymouth horizon miser	38.0	4	105.0	63	2125	14.7	82	US
373	mercury lynx l	36.0	4	98.0	70	2125	17.3	82	US
381	oldsmobile cutlass ciera (diesel)	38.0	6	262.0	85	3015	17.0	82	US
385	dodge charger 2.2	36.0	4	135.0	84	2370	13.0	82	US

Finally, we can create a new column in the DataFrame that the data is saved in.

```
cars_df['MPG_per_cylinder']=cars_df['MPG']/cars_df['Cylinders']
```

Further Readings

For more information about Pandas, you can go here:
https://pandas.pydata.org/pandas-docs/stable/

2.7. Matplotlib

Matplotlib is the fundamental library in Python for plotting 2D and even some 3D data. You can use it to plot many different plots, such as histograms, bar plots, heatmaps, line plots, scatter plots, and many others.

Let us see how to work with it. We start by importing it.

```
import matplotlib.pyplot as plt
import numpy as np
```

Then, we generate some random data to plot.

```
x = np.arange(10)
y = 4*x + 5 + np.random.random(size=x.size)
print(x)
print(y)
[0 1 2 3 4 5 6 7 8 9]
[5.55702208  9.05720778  13.01066085  17.02045126  21.69267435
25.80298672  29.917964  33.16520441  37.12348891  41.62939263]
```

After that, we plot using the scatter method.

```
plt.scatter(x, y)
```

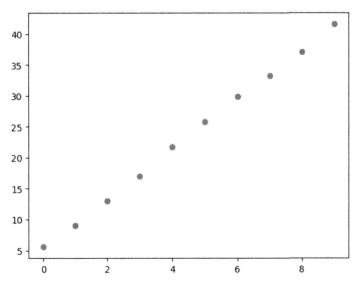

We can make the plot more beautiful.

```
# Use `o` as marker; color set as `r` (red); size proportion
to Y values
plt.scatter(x, y, marker='+', c='r', s=y*10)
# How about adding a line to it? Let's use `plt.plot()`
# set line style to dashed; color as `k` (black)
plt.plot(x, y, linestyle='dashed', color='k')
# set x/y axis limits: first two are xlow and xhigh; last two
are ylow and yhigh
plt.axis([0, 10, 0, 35])
# set x/y labels
plt.xlabel('My X Axis')
plt.ylabel('My Y Axis')
# set title
plt.title('My First Plot')
```

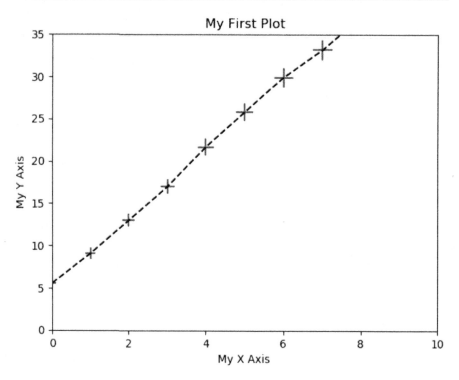

Let us understand the anatomy of the figure by the following figure.

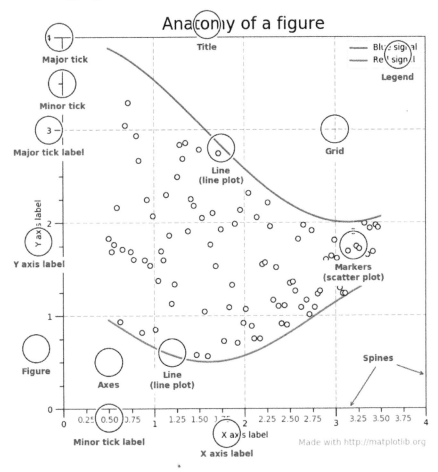

We can also have many sub-plots as follows.

```
# Now the returned `ax` would be array with a shape a 2x2
fig, ax_arr = plt.subplots(nrows=2, ncols=2)

# Now the returned `ax` would be an array with a shape a 2x2
for ax_row in ax_arr:
    for ax in ax_row:
ax.plot(x, y)
```

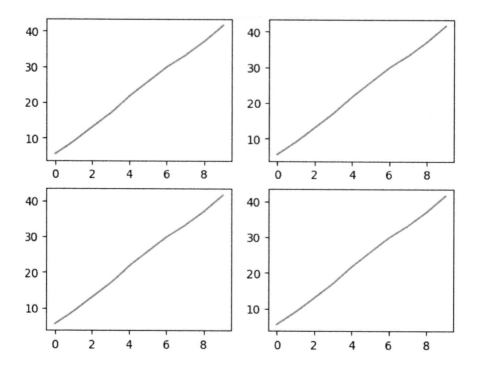

Now, let us use the visualization on a real dataset to enhance our understanding. We will be using the cars dataset once again.

We start by importing the libraries, fixing the path, and loading the dataset.

```
import pandas as pd
import os
os.chdir('D:')
os.getcwd()
cars_df=pd.read_excel('cars.xls')
```

Then, we simply call the scatter method and pass our dataset variables.

```
plt.figure(figsize=(15,10))
plt.scatter(cars_df.Horsepower,cars_df.MPG,c=cars_
df.Year,s=cars_df.Displacement, alpha=0.5)
plt.xlabel(r'Horsepower', fontsize=15)
plt.ylabel(r'MPG', fontsize=15)
plt.title('MPG vs Horsepower by Year and Displacement',
fontsize=25)
plt.show()
```

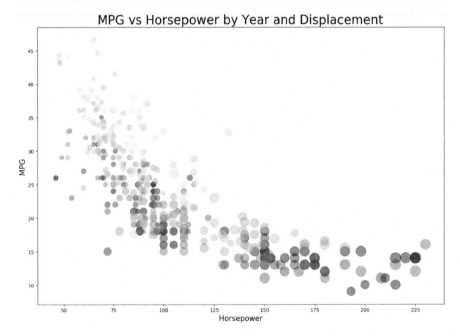

Now, let us experiment and see different kinds of plots, which are the histograms, the boxplot, the bar plot, and the line plot. We will start with the **histogram**.

Let us create some random data with Gaussian distribution.

```
mu, sigma = 15, 1
gaussian_arr=np.random.normal(mu,sigma,size=10000)
np.mean(gaussian_arr), np.std(gaussian_arr, ddof=1)
(14.990546050758532, 1.0051987624650212)
```

Now, let us plot this data using a histogram.

```
fig, ax = plt.subplots()
freq_arr, bin_arr, _ = ax.hist(gaussian_arr)
```

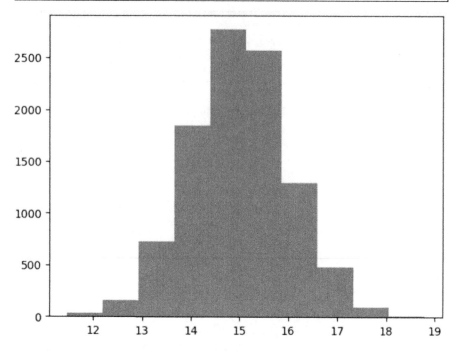

Then, we try to make it look better.

```
fig, ax = plt.subplots()
# Facecolor set to green; transparency (`alpha`) level: 30%
freq_arr,bin_arr,_=ax.hist(gaussian_arr,facecolor='g',
alpha=0.3)
# Add grid
ax.grid()
```

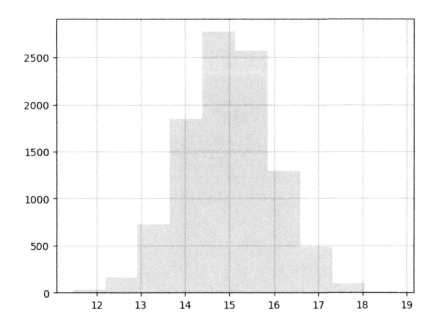

After that, we repeat the same code but on our cars' dataset.

```
cars_df.MPG.hist()
plt.show()
```

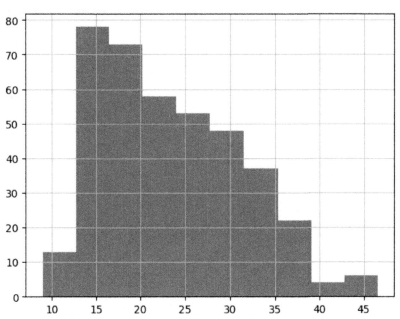

We then use the same data but using a **boxplot**.

```
fig, ax = plt.subplots()
ax.boxplot(gaussian_arr,
           vert=False,  #verticle
showfliers=False, # do not show outliers
showmeans=True, # show the mean
           labels=['Gaussian'] # group name (label)
           )
```

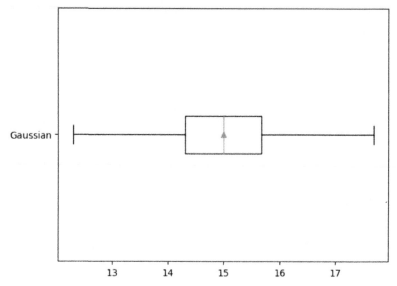

From there, we can experiment with **the bar plots** and see how they look and are used. Here, we combine them with error bars that are frequently used when we have uncertainty about our data.

```
bar_arr = np.array(['Spring', 'Summer', 'Fall', 'Winder'])
freq_arr = np.random.randint(0, 100, 4)
yerr_arr = np.random.randint(5, 10, 4)
```

```
fig, ax = plt.subplots()
ax.bar(bar_arr, freq_arr, # X and Y
yerr = yerr_arr, # error bars
       color='red',
       )
```

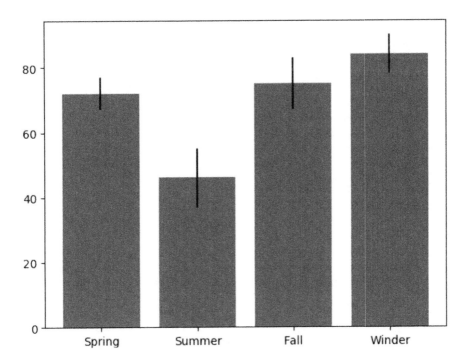

The last type of plot that we are going to mention is the **line plot**. We will artificially generate the data with the following distribution so they can be interpreted easily in the plots.

```
dt = 0.01
t = np.arange(0, 30, dt)
nse1 = np.random.randn(len(t))
nse2 = np.random.randn(len(t))
r = np.exp(-t / 0.05)
cnse1 = np.convolve(nse1, r, mode='same') * dt
cnse2 = np.convolve(nse2, r, mode='same') * dt
s1 = 0.01 * np.sin(2 * np.pi * 10 * t) + cnse1
s2 = 0.01 * np.sin(2 * np.pi * 10 * t) + cnse2
```

Now, we can create two plots in one plot using the sub-plots function.

```
fig, (ax1, ax2) = plt.subplots(2, 1)
# make a little extra space between the subplots
fig.subplots_adjust(hspace=0.5)
ax1.plot(t, s1, t, s2)
ax1.set_xlim(0, 5)
ax1.set_xlabel('time')
ax1.set_ylabel('s1 and s2')
ax1.grid(True)
cxy, f = ax2.csd(s1, s2, 256, 1. / dt)
ax2.set_ylabel('CSD (db)')
plt.show()
```

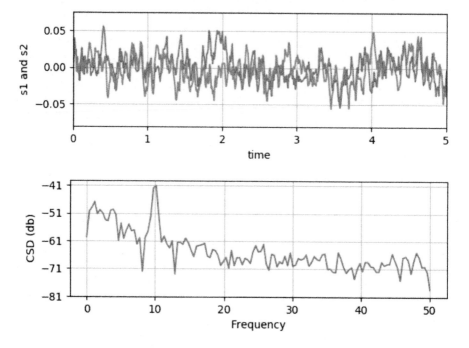

Finally, we can combine the four different types of plots that we discussed in a single plot.

```
fig, ax_arr = plt.subplots(nrows=2, ncols=2,sharex=False,
sharey=False)
fig.set_figwidth(12)
fig.set_figheight(8)
# set global title
fig.suptitle("My first subplots")
## first
ax_arr[0, 0].scatter(x, y, marker='+', c='g', s=y*10)
ax_arr[0, 0].plot(x, y, linestyle='dashed', color='k')
ax_arr[0, 0].axis([0, 10, 0, 35])
ax_arr[0, 0].set_title('My First Plot')
## second
ax_arr[0, 1].hist(gaussian_arr, facecolor='g', alpha=0.3)
ax_arr[0, 1].set_title('Histogram')
## third
ax_arr[1, 0].boxplot(gaussian_arr, vert=False, showfliers=False,
showmeans=True, labels=['Gaussian'])
ax_arr[1, 0].set_title('Box plot')
## last one
ax_arr[1,1].bar(bar_arr, freq_arr,
yerr = yerr_arr, color='gold')
ax_arr[1, 1].set_title('Bar chart')
```

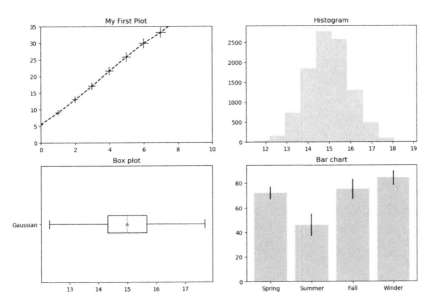

One final thing before we move on. It is worth mentioning that there is another less used library called **seaborn**, which can help us have some good-looking graphs.

```
import seaborn as sns
sns.heatmap(cars_df.corr())
plt.show()
```

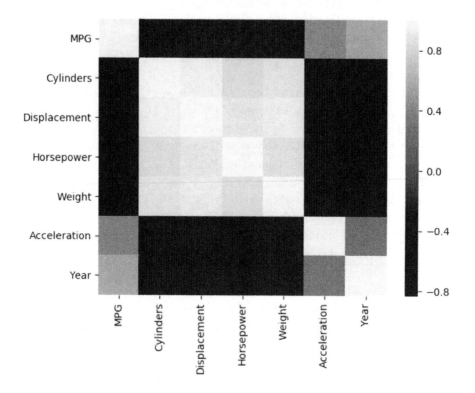

Further Readings

For more information about Matplotlib, you can get back to this tutorial here.

2.8. SciPy

SciPy is a very important library for linear algebra operations, it is and also used in Fourier Transformers.

While it is a low-level library compared to other libraries that we will use, it is important to get familiar with it because you may need to develop your algorithm from scratch, and this library will be of use then.

Note that the SciPy library depends on NumPy for all its operations.

Let us see how to compute 10^x using SciPy.

```
import scipy
```

SciPy also gives functionality to calculate permutations and combinations.

```
from scipy.special import exp10
exp = exp10([1,10])
print(exp)
[1.e+01 1.e+10]
```

We can also determine the determinant of a two-dimensional matrix.

```
from scipy.special import comb,perm
com = comb(5, 2, exact = False)
per=perm(5, 2, exact=False)
print(com)
print(per)
10.0
20.0
```

Finally, for our discussion, let us calculate the inverse of any matrix using SciPy:

```
scipy.linalg.inv(two_d_array)
array([[-0.28571429,  0.71428571],
       [0.42857143, -0.57142857]])
```

SciPy will not be used that much in our discussions, as we will use more high-level libraries to compute the determinant and other operations. However, it is good to know.

> **Further Readings**
>
> For more information about SciPy, you can get back to this tutorial here.

2.9. Statsmodels

Given that this book focuses on one of the fundamental statistical methods, we will be using Statsmodels library to understand the details of regression analysis. Statsmodels is a Python library that provides many functions that help to estimate many different statistical models, along with conducting tactical tests and statistical data exploration.

Let us see a very basic example of what Statsmodels can offer. While we will not go into details about what each line means right now, we will see how powerful this library is.

```
import numpy as np
import statsmodels.api as sp
import statsmodels.formula.api as smf
dat=sm.datasets.get_rdataset("Guerry","HistData").data
results=smf.ols('Lottery~Literacy+np.log(Pop1831)',data =
dat).fit()
```

Here, we are using a dummy dataset and doing a type of regression analysis called Ordinary Least Squares regression, which we will discuss later. As you can see, this can be done using only one line of code.

Then, using only one line of code, we can get the result of dozens of statistical tests very easily.

```
print(results.summary())
```

```
                            OLS Regression Results
==============================================================================
Dep. Variable:                Lottery   R-squared:                       0.348
Model:                            OLS   Adj. R-squared:                  0.333
Method:                 Least Squares   F-statistic:                     22.20
Date:                Sun, 24 Nov 2019   Prob (F-statistic):           1.90e-08
Time:                        07:54:32   Log-Likelihood:                -379.82
No. Observations:                  86   AIC:                             765.6
Df Residuals:                      83   BIC:                             773.0
Df Model:                           2
Covariance Type:            nonrobust
==============================================================================
                   coef    std err          t      P>|t|      [0.025      0.975]
------------------------------------------------------------------------------
Intercept        246.4341     35.233      6.995      0.000     176.358     316.510
Literacy          -0.4889      0.128     -3.832      0.000      -0.743      -0.235
np.log(Pop1831)  -31.3114      5.977     -5.239      0.000     -43.199     -19.424
==============================================================================
Omnibus:                        3.713   Durbin-Watson:                   2.019
Prob(Omnibus):                  0.156   Jarque-Bera (JB):                3.394
Skew:                          -0.487   Prob(JB):                        0.183
Kurtosis:                       3.003   Cond. No.                        702.
==============================================================================
```

2.10. Scikit-Learn

Let us now introduce one of the most important libraries for anyone starting to learn machine learning, Sklearn, or Scikit-Learn.

This library includes out-of-the-box ready-to-use machine learning algorithms. It literary has most of the algorithms that we will talk about in this eBook. The beautiful thing about it is that it has very great documentation. But more than that, it is very simple and intuitive to use. We will look at how to use this library to do all kinds of regression analysis in this book, starting from chapter 3.

The library also provides many utilities for data-preprocessing and data visualization and evaluation.

We start by importing the modules that we will use from sklearn.

```
from sklearn.linear_model import LinearRegression
from sklearn.model_selection import train_test_split
```

Then we call the algorithm that we will use, which is the linear regression.

```
lm=LinearRegression()
```

After that, we load the cars' dataset to work with.

```
import pandas as pd
import os
os.chdir('D:')
os.getcwd()
cars_df=pd.read_excel('cars.xls')
cars_df.head()
```

	Model	MPG	Cylinders	Displacement	Horsepower	Weight	Acceleration	Year	Origin
0	chevroletchevellemalibu	18.0	8	307.0	130	3504	12.0	70	US
1	buick skylark 320	15.0	8	350.0	165	3693	11.5	70	US
2	plymouth satellite	18.0	8	318.0	150	3436	11.0	70	US
3	amc rebel sst	16.0	8	304.0	150	3433	12.0	70	US
4	ford torino	17.0	8	302.0	140	3449	10.5	70	US

Following that, we choose x to be all the dataset variables without the origin, the model, and the MPG columns. Also, we choose y to be the output variable, which is MPG. Moreover, we drop any missing values.

```
x=cars_df.dropna().drop(columns=['MPG','Model','Origin'])
y= cars_df.dropna().MPG
```

Then, we split our dataset into training and testing.

```
X_train,X_test,y_train,y_test=train_test_split(x,y,
test_size=0.3,random_state=42)
```

We then fit the model and predict the output. We will understand all the details in chapter 3.

```
lm.fit(X_train,y_train)
lm.predict(X_test)
```

Finally, we will plot the data with the predicted outputs.

```python
# add your actual vs. predicted points
plt.scatter(y_test, lm.predict(X_test))
# add the line of perfect fit
straight_line = np.arange(0, 60)
plt.plot(straight_line, straight_line)
plt.title("Fitted Values")
plt.show()
```

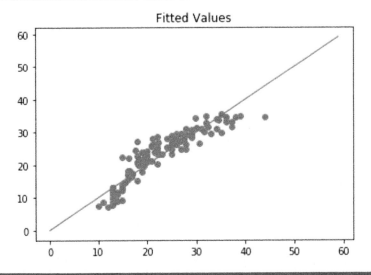

Fitted Values

Further Readings

For more information about Sklearn, you can go to https://scikit-learn.org/stable/documentation.html.

2.11. Summary and Exercises

To summarize, in this chapter, we got hands-on experience with Python and many of its powerful data science libraries. We started with installing Python and understanding its syntax. Then, we dived into the details of Python data structures. After that, we introduced a lot of libraries and tools that we will use throughout the book, such as NumPy, Pandas, Matplotlib, and others.

If you want to start working on the exercises, try to implement everything we discussed yourself. Also, explore the other default options of all the functions we used and see how the results will change.

3

Data Preparation

I can tell you from personal experience that 80 percent to 90 percent of the time devoted to any data science or machine learning project is spent on data exploration, preparation, and preprocessing. Thus, in this chapter, we will focus on these concepts, as they are not only crucial for regression, but also for any accurate statistical analysis or machine learning algorithms.

3.1. Missing Data

After loading the data in a Python DataFrame, the first step of data preprocessing is to check if there are any missing data. That is because having missing values in your dataset will lead to various problems while doing the next steps of preprocessing and even in your final regression analysis.

Detecting missing values in Python is very simple. If we have our data in a DataFrame called df, for example, we can detect all missing values using the following line of code.

```
df.isnull()
```

That was easy! However, the tricky part is how should we deal with missing values?

There is no definite answer. But rather, some options that you choose from or combine, based on your needs, as it is more of an art than science.

The options that can fit in a regression analysis can be summarized as follows:

1. Filling them (imputation)
2. Deleting them
3. Use machine learning to predict the missing values.

The third option is out of the scope of this book. However, you can try it yourself once you have a solid understanding of the machine learning algorithms.

The deletion option should be done with caution. We usually do this if we have an entire observation or row with missing values, which means that most probably, this observation was corrupted during data collection, or there is a mistake with it. If we have a dataset with 100,000 observations and only 100 of them are nearly or completely missing, then we can delete these observations confidently, as they represent only 0.1percent of the data.

The imputation option by itself can be broken down into many options as follows:

1. Mean or median substitution
2. Most frequent
3. Replace with −1 or −9999

The pros and cons can be summarized as follows:

Method	Pros	Cons
Mean/Median	• Easy and Fast. • Works well with small numerical values	• Works only on columns level. • Poor results with encoded categorical features. • Not accurate enough.
Most Frequent	• Works well with categorical variables.	• May introduce bias in the data. • Works only on columns level.
Replace with a constant	• Works well with categorical variables.	• Basic method

Let us see how to handle missing values in Python.

First, let us detect the missing values. We will do so by first importing the needed libraries and the Dataset.

```
import numpy as np
import pandas as pd
fords=pd.read_csv('fords.csv')
```

Then, let us explore our dataset by printing out the first five columns.

```
fords.head()
```

	Year	Mileage	Price	Color	Location	Model	Age
0	1990	NaN	1600.0	NaN	Phoenix	NaN	19
1	1994	94000.0	1988.0	white	Phoenix	GL	15
2	1995	NaN	2288.0	white	Phoenix	NaN	14
3	1995	68000.0	2495.0	NaN	Phoenix	NaN	14
4	1995	NaN	1995.0	NaN	Phoenix	GL	14

Then, we can get more information about the DataFrame using the following two methods.

```
fords.info()
<class 'pandas.core.frame.DataFrame'>
RangeIndex: 635 entries, 0 to 634
Data columns (total 7 columns):
Year        635 non-null int64
Mileage     616 non-null float64
Price       629 non-null float64
Color       625 non-null object
Location    635 non-null object
Model       627 non-null object
Age         635 non-null int64
dtypes: float64(2), int64(2), object(3)
memory usage: 34.8+ KB
```

```
fords.describe()
```

	Year	Mileage	Price	Age
count	635.000000	616.000000	6.290000e+02	635.000000
mean	2004.886614	56015.571429	2.531353e+04	4.280315
std	4.989553	34145.828077	3.983778e+05	3.284152
min	1990.000000	42.000000	1.200000e+03	0.000000
25%	2003.000000	31772.750000	5.995000e+03	2.000000
50%	2006.000000	48897.500000	8.950000e+03	3.000000
75%	2007.000000	74503.250000	1.169000e+04	6.000000
max	2100.000000	181484.000000	9.999999e+06	19.000000

As we see, there are many missing values in some of the features in the dataset, such as price and mileage.

To make sure of this, we can use the *isna* function found in the Pandas library.

```
fords.isna()
```

	Year	Mileage	Price	Color	Location	Model	Age
0	False	True	False	True	False	True	False
1	False	False	False	False	False	False	False

Then, we can drop the missing values.

```
fords.dropna(inplace=True)
fords.info()
<class 'pandas.core.frame.DataFrame'>
Int64Index: 599 entries, 1 to 634
Data columns (total 7 columns):
Year         599 non-null int64
Mileage      599 non-null float64
Price        599 non-null float64
Color        599 non-null object
Location     599 non-null object
Model        599 non-null object
Age          599 non-null int64
dtypes: float64(2), int64(2), object(3)
memory usage: 37.4+ KB
```

As we can see, using this method results in dropping all the rows that have even one missing value.

Now, let us impute the missing values with the mean value. To do so, we will use a function from Sklearn library as follows:

```
from sklearn.impute import SimpleImputer
fords=pd.read_csv('fords.csv')
fords = fords[['Year','Mileage','Price','Age']]
```

We chose only the numerical variables as this method is not recommended with categorical variables. Now, let us see how to use it.

```
imp_mean = SimpleImputer(strategy='mean') #for median
imputation replace 'mean' with 'median', and for most frequent
replace it with 'most_frequent'
imr_mean = imr_mean.fit(fords[[Mileage]])
fords[Mileage]=
imr_mean.transform(fords[[Mileage]]).ravel()
fords.info()
<class 'pandas.core.frame.DataFrame'>
RangeIndex: 635 entries, 0 to 634
Data columns (total 4 columns):
Year        635 non-null int64
Mileage     635 non-null float64
Price       629 non-null float64
Age         635 non-null int64
dtypes: float64(2), int64(2)
memory usage: 19.9 KB
```

As we see, we filled the missing values in the mileage feature with the average value of the whole feature.

Finally, let us see how we can replace missing values with a constant such as−9999.

```
fords=pd.read_csv('fords.csv')
fords.fillna(-9999,inplace=True)
fords.info()
<class 'pandas.core.frame.DataFrame'>
RangeIndex: 635 entries, 0 to 634
Data columns (total 7 columns):
Year        635 non-null int64
Mileage     635 non-null float64
Price       635 non-null float64
Color       635 non-null object
Location    635 non-null object
Model       635 non-null object
Age         635 non-null int64
dtypes: float64(2), int64(2), object(3)
memory usage: 34.8+ KB
```

3.2. Outliers

The second step in cleaning the data is to detect and remove any outliers. But first, what is meant exactly by outliers?

We can frankly say that any data point that is very different from the rest of the data points can be considered as an outlier. This is not a solid or a scientific definition, but it can give you an idea about what outliers mean.

For the scientific definition of outliers, we need to understand what is meant by quartiles. If we have 100 observations in our dataset, we can divide it into four quarters. If the values of the dataset are [1, 2, 3, ..., 99, 100], then we can say that the first quartile Q1 is 25, the second quartile Q2 is 50, the third quartile Q3 is 75, right?

But if the dataset does not have this distribution, then we calculate Q1 as the median of the lower half of the data, and Q3 as the median of the upper half of the data.

Suppose we have the following numbers [1, 2, 5, 6, 7, 9, 12, 15, 18, 19, 27], we arrange them, and we find the median which is **9**. Then, we split the data into two parts (1, 2, 5, 6, 7), 9, (12, 15, 18, 19, 27). Now, it is obvious that the median of Q1 is **5**, while that of Q3 is **18**.

We can define the following definitions out of the quartiles:

1. lower inner fence: Q1 − 1.5*IQ
2. upper inner fence: Q3 + 1.5*IQ
3. lower outer fence: Q1 − 3*IQ
4. upper outer fence: Q3 + 3*IQ

Now, for the scientific definition of the outliers, any data points that are present beyond an inner fence on either side are considered **mild outliers,** and any data points that are beyond an outer fence are considered **extreme outliers.**

There are two frequently used ways to detect outliers in Python, which are box plots and histograms. Both were discussed in the last chapter. Let us see how to use it with a real-world dataset.

```
fords=pd.read_csv('fords.csv')
fords.Year.hist()
plt.show()
```

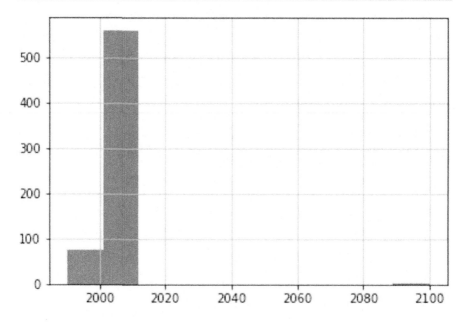

We were able to detect some outliers. Now, let us remove them.

```
fords = fords[fords.Year<2090]
fords.Year.hist()
plt.show()
```

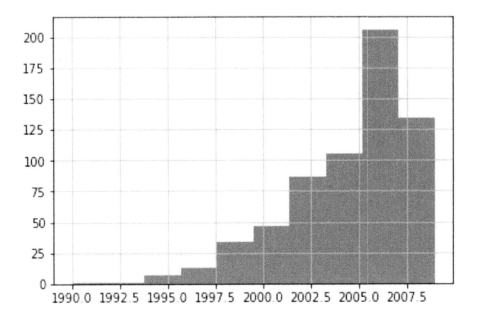

Now, let us try to do the same with a box plot.

```
fords=pd.read_csv('fords.csv')
fig1, ax1 = plt.subplots()
ax1.boxplot(fords.Year)
```

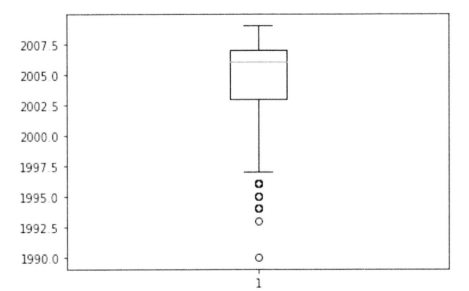

```
fords = fords[fords.Year<2090]
fig1, ax1 = plt.subplots()
ax1.boxplot(fords.Year)
```

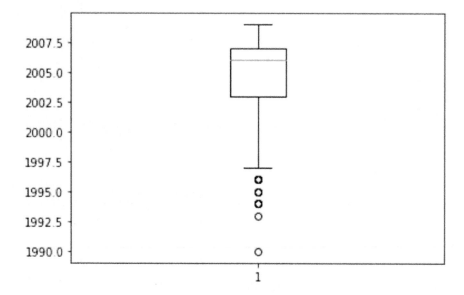

3.3. Standardization

The third step in data preprocessing is standardization, or mean removal and variance scaling. This is a crucial requirement for most of the machine learning algorithms, including regression analysis. This is because these algorithms assume that the features look like standard normally distributed data, which is a **Gaussian** with zero mean μ and unit variance σ^2.

We can see the plot of different Gaussian distributions in the following figure. We need to convert the distribution of the dataset's features to be as close as possible to the red graph.

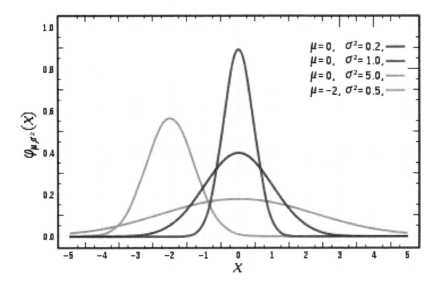

To do so in Python, we transform the data by removing the mean value of each feature and then scale them by dividing non-constant features by their standard deviation.

Let us see how to do this in practice.

```
from sklearn import preprocessing
import numpy as np
X_train = np.array([[ 1., -1.,  2.],
                    [ 2.,  0.,  0.],
                    [ 0.,  1., -1.]])
X_scaled = preprocessing.scale(X_train)
print(X_scaled)
array([[ 0.  ..., -1.22..., 1.33...],
       [ 1.22...,  0.  ..., -0.26...],
       [-1.22...,  1.22..., -1.06...]])
```

Let us see the mean and the variance of the data after standardization.

```
print(X_scaled.mean(axis=0))
print(X_scaled.std(axis=0))
array([0., 0., 0.])
array([1., 1., 1.])
```

Another technique to standardize the dataset is to compute the mean and the variance and apply them to any part of the data. Sklearn can help us to do so also using the following code.

We start by importing the needed libraries and loading the dataset. Then, we apply the standard scaler function found in Sklearn and fit it on the dataset. After that, we see the mean values of the four variables.

```
import numpy as np
import pandas as pd
import sklearn.preprocessing as preprocessing
fords=pd.read_csv('fords.csv')
fords = fords[['Year','Mileage','Price','Age']]
scaler = preprocessing.StandardScaler().fit(fords)
print(scaler.mean_)
[2.00488661e+03 5.60155714e+04 2.53135326e+04 4.28031496e+00]
```

We can also print the standard deviation of the dataset.

```
print(scaler.scale_)
[4.98562283e+00 3.41181011e+04 3.98060973e+05 3.28156481e+00]
```

Finally, we can apply this transformation on the dataset to standardize it.

```
print(scaler.transform(fords))
[[ 1.90775334e+01  2.66560640e+00 -5.60681255e-02
3.26663822e+00]
 [-1.78244815e+00  3.44797703e+00 -5.85702548e-02
2.65717288e+00]
 [ 6.24472796e-01 -1.46914892e+00 -1.71846352e-02
-9.99619129e-01]]
```

3.4. Normalization

Another important step in data preprocessing is normalization, which is the process of scaling individual observations to have unit norm. It is very important in regression analysis to have the same weights for each feature in the dataset.

For instance, suppose we want to predict the price of a house based on several features. One of these features can be the number of bedrooms, while another one can be the area of the house. The problem now is that the range of values for the bedroom's variable is not on the same scale as the other variable. Thus, even though they can be equally important in our estimation of the price, the second variable mathematically will have a much bigger influence on the final estimation. That is why we need to normalize the dataset before we do any analysis.

Note the difference between standardization and normalization. The first one tries to distribute the data equally without changing the range of the values for each variable independently, while the second one tries to make all the values in the whole dataset on the same range.

There are a lot of mathematical tricks that can be used to convert to normalize the dataset. The most famous ones are the *l2 norm* and the *l1 norm*. We will not go into the mathematics behind them, but rather will see how to use them in Python.

```
X = [[ 1., -1.,  2.],
     [ 2.,  0.,  0.],
     [ 0.,  1., -1.]]
X_normalized = preprocessing.normalize(X, norm='l2')
print(X_normalized)
array([[ 0.40..., -0.40...,  0.81...],
       [ 1.  ...,  0.  ...,  0.  ...],
       [ 0.  ...,  0.70..., -0.70...]])
```

As we can see, all the values are now in the range between zero and 1.

3.5. **Summarization by Binning**

The last preprocessing step that we can do with numerical variables is summarization, which is a way to partition continuous variables into discrete values. This can help in certain cases as this discretization process can transform the dataset of continuous values to only one with nominal attributes.

Moreover, using binning can make the regression model more expressive without losing its interpretability by introducing non-linearity to a linear model, for example.

There are two main methods for binning, which are **K-bins** and **Feature Binarization**.

K-bins summarization works by discretizing features into k bins. Let us see an example.

```
X = np.array([[ -3., 5., 15 ],
[  0., 6., 14 ],
[  6., 3., 11 ]])
est = preprocessing.KBinsDiscretizer(n_bins=[3, 2, 2],
encode='ordinal').fit(X)
print(est.transform(X))
[[0. 1. 1.]
 [1. 1. 1.]
 [2. 0. 0.]]
```

What happened is that we defined three bins for the first feature, two bins for the second feature, and two bins for the last feature. Then, we fitted the model on our tiny dataset. Finally, when we applied our transformation on the dataset, we got the discretized results. We observe that the first column has only values from 0 to 2, because we defined only three bins for this column, and the transformed values follow the same distribution of the original values.

Feature binarization, on the other hand, works by having thresholds on the numerical values to have either 0 or 1 for each value. This can be extremely useful in applications such as text analysis and processing. However, it is not commonly used in regression analysis.

Let us see an example.

```
X = [[ 1., -1.,  2.],
     [ 2.,  0.,  0.],
     [ 0.,  1., -1.]]
binarizer = preprocessing.Binarizer()
print(binarizer.transform(X))
[[1. 0. 1.]
 [1. 0. 0.]
 [0. 1. 0.]]
```

As we can see, all the values now are either 0 or 1 based on the mathematical methods that are used in the binarization function.

3.6. Qualitative Features Encoding

So far, we have tackled preprocessing for variables that contain numbers, which we call **quantitative** variables. However, we did not tackle, yet, how to deal with variables that have strings, which is called **qualitative** variables or categorical variables.

We can say that the data are categorical if the different values that the data can have cannot be used in mathematical operations. Categorical data can be split even more to **ordinal** (ordered) data and **nominal** (unordered) data. The rating of a movie is a good example of ordinal categorical data, while blood type is a good example of nominal data.

On the other hand, numerical data can be used in mathematical operations. Numerical data can be split even more to **discrete** numerical data and **continuous** numerical data. Discrete numerical data can only have one of a pre-defined set of values—examples of what can be the number of bedrooms in a house. Continuous data can have any value from negative infinity to infinity—examples of what can be the speed of a car. But of course, depending on the nature of the variable in the data, even the continuous variables should be restricted by a range.

So, all the techniques that we discussed so far will not work on the categorical variables with their original state. Thus, we need to manipulate them one way or another so all that we discussed can be used.

This can be done by encoding the categorical variables into numbers. There are two main ways to do so using Sklearn, which are **Ordinal Encoding** and **One-Hot Encoding**. Let us see how to use both.

```
enc=preprocessing.OrdinalEncoder()
X = [['male', 'from US', 'uses Safari'], ['female', 'from
Europe', 'uses Firefox']]
enc.fit(X)
print(enc.transform([['female', 'from US', 'uses Safari']]))
print(enc.transform([['male', 'from US', 'uses Firefox']]))
[[0. 1. 1.]]
[[1. 1. 0.]]
```

We used the ordinal encoder found in Sklearn by first defining it and fitting it into our tiny dataset. Then we applied this fitted encoder on different examples. For the first one, we got 0 1 1 as the female was encoded as 1 while the male was decoded as 0, and so on.

Now, let us see how to use one-hot encoding, on a tiny dataset also.

```
enc = preprocessing.OneHotEncoder()
X = [['male', 'from US', 'uses Safari'], ['female', 'from
Europe', 'uses Firefox']]
enc.fit(X)
print(enc.transform([['female', 'from US', 'uses Safari'],
['male', 'from Europe', 'usesSafari']]).toarray())
[[1. 0. 0. 1. 0. 1.]
 [0. 1. 1. 0. 0. 1.]]
```

Ok, let us understand how one-hot encoding, which is also called a dummy or one-of-K encoding, works by walking through the previous code snippet.

We performed the same steps of ordinal encoding but got different results. That is because one-hot encoding works by transforming each categorical variable with n possible values into n binary features, where one of them equals 1 and all others equal 0.

In our case, we have only two possible values for each categorical variable. Therefore, the male was encoded 0 1 and female was encoded 1 0, from the US was encoded 0 1 and from Europe was encoded 1 0, uses Firefox was encoded 0 1 and uses Safari was encoded 1 0.

Now, we can decode 1 0 0 1 0 1, which will be female from the US uses Safari.

3.7. Dummy Coding with Pandas

As we saw, dealing with categorical variables can be tricky and exhausting. You might be wondering, should we know all the possible values for each variable to encode them as we did in the last section? The answer is NO. We can use Pandas function called *get_dummies* to interpret the categorical variables and deal with them automatically.

Let us see how it works.

```
df = pd.DataFrame({'sex': ['male','female'], 'country': ['from
US','from Europe'], 'browser': ['uses Safari','Uses Firefox'],
'numerical': [1, 2]})
df.head()
```

	sex	country	browser	numerical
0	male	from US	uses Safari	1
1	female	from Europe	Uses Firefox	2

As we can see, this dataset can contain any values. In fact, at the end of this chapter, we will use pandas to detect and encode categorical variables from a real-world dataset as a part of the preprocessing pipeline.

If you noticed, I have intentionally inserted a numerical variable to emphasize that this function transforms only the categorical variables.

```
pd.get_dummies(df)
```

	numerical	sex_female	sex_male	country_from Europe	country_from US	browser_Uses Firefox	browser_uses Safari
0	1	0	1	0	1	0	1
1	2	1	0	1	0	1	0

That was easy!

3.8. Summary

To summarize, in this chapter, we have explored different tricks of data preparation, such as dealing with missing values, dealing with outliers, standardizing the dataset, scaling the variables, and different techniques to encode categorical variables.

Data preparation is, as we said before, an exhausting task and can take a lot of the time allocated for the project. However, it is a necessary step to get any reliable results that you can build conclusions upon.

In the following section, we will see how we can do all this on a real-world dataset.

3.9. Hands-On Project

Finally, let us examine how we can apply all the tricks we have learned on a real-world dataset.

We start by importing all the libraries that we need and load our dataset.

```
import numpy as np
import pandas as pd
import sklearn.preprocessing as preprocessing
from sklearn.impute import SimpleImputer
import matplotlib.pyplot as plt
```

```
fords=pd.read_csv('fords.csv')
fords.head()
```

	Year	Mileage	Price	Color	Location	Model	Age
0	1990	NaN	1600.0	NaN	Phoenix	NaN	19
1	1994	94000.0	1988.0	white	Phoenix	GL	15
2	1995	NaN	2288.0	white	Phoenix	NaN	14
3	1995	68000.0	2495.0	NaN	Phoenix	NaN	14
4	1995	NaN	1995.0	NaN	Phoenix	GL	14

We print some information and statistics about the dataset to observe that we have some missing values and some outliers.

```
fords.info()
<class 'pandas.core.frame.DataFrame'>
RangeIndex: 635 entries, 0 to 634
Data columns (total 7 columns):
Year         635 non-null int64
Mileage      616 non-null float64
Price        629 non-null float64
Color        625 non-null object
Location     635 non-null object
Model        627 non-null object
Age          635 non-null int64
dtypes: float64(2), int64(2), object(3)
memory usage: 34.8+ KB
```

```
fords.describe()
```

	Year	Mileage	Price	Age
count	635.000000	616.000000	6.290000e+02	635.000000
mean	2004.886614	56015.571429	2.531353e+04	4.280315
std	4.989553	34145.828077	3.983778e+05	3.284152
min	1990.000000	42.000000	1.200000e+03	0.000000
25%	2003.000000	31772.750000	5.995000e+03	2.000000
50%	2006.000000	48897.500000	8.950000e+03	3.000000
75%	2007.000000	74503.250000	1.169000e+04	6.000000
max	2100.000000	181484.000000	9.999999e+06	19.000000

We start by encoding the categorical features to be dummy variables.

```
# Encoding
fords= pd.get_dummies(fords)
fords.head()
```

	Year	Mileage	Price	Age	Color_beige	Color_black	Color_blue	Color_brown	Color_burgundy	Color_gold	...
0	1990	NaN	1600.0	19	0	0	0	0	0	0	...
1	1994	94000.0	1988.0	15	0	0	0	0	0	0	...
2	1995	NaN	2288.0	14	0	0	0	0	0	0	...
3	1995	68000.0	2495.0	14	0	0	0	0	0	0	...
4	1995	NaN	1995.0	14	0	0	0	0	0	0	...

5 rows × 26 columns

Then, we impute the missing values with the average value of each column.

```
#missing
rows=['Year','Mileage','Price','Age']
for numerical_row in rows:
imr_mean = SimpleImputer(strategy='mean')
imr_mean = imr_mean.fit(fords[[numerical_row]])
    fords[numerical_row] = imr_mean.
transform(fords[[numerical_row]]).ravel()


fords.info()
<class 'pandas.core.frame.DataFrame'>
RangeIndex: 635 entries, 0 to 634
Data columns (total 26 columns):
Year                    635 non-null float64
Mileage                 635 non-null float64
Price                   635 non-null float64
Age                     635 non-null float64
Color_beige             635 non-null uint8
Color_black             635 non-null uint8
Color_blue              635 non-null uint8
Color_brown             635 non-null uint8
Color_burgundy          635 non-null uint8
```

After that, we plot a histogram to detect outliers in different features.

```
#outliers
fords.Year.hist()
plt.show()
```

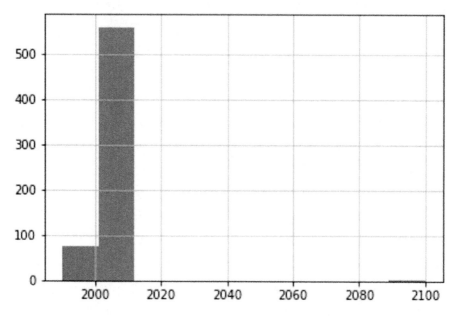

```
fords.Mileage.hist()
plt.show()
```

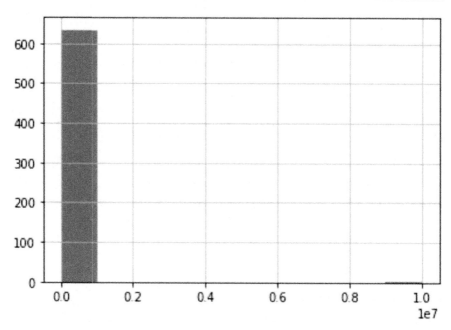

We then remove the outliers using the following line.

```
fords=fords.loc[~((fords.Price>8000000)|
                  (fords.Year>2080)),]
```

The next step is to standardize the numerical variables.

```
# Standardization
scaler = preprocessing.MinMaxScaler()
fords[['Year','Mileage','Price','Age']] = scaler.fit_
transform(fords[['Year','Mileage',
'Price','Age']])
fords.head()
```

	Year	Mileage	Price	Age	Color_beige	Color_black
0	0.000000	0.308493	0.016588	1.000000	0	0
1	0.210526	0.517840	0.032679	0.789474	0	0
2	0.263158	0.308493	0.045120	0.736842	0	0
3	0.263158	0.374544	0.053704	0.736842	0	0
4	0.263158	0.308493	0.032969	0.736842	0	0

5 rows × 26 columns

Now, let us normalize the numerical features.

```
#normalization
fords[['Year','Mileage','Price','Age']] = preprocessing.
normalize(fords[[
    'Year','Mileage','Price','Age']])
fords.head()
```

	Year	Mileage	Price	Age	Color_beige	Color_black
0	0.000000	0.294748	0.015849	0.955444	0	0
1	0.217510	0.535018	0.033763	0.815662	0	0
2	0.312445	0.366271	0.053570	0.874845	0	0
3	0.302789	0.430950	0.061792	0.847810	0	0
4	0.312654	0.366516	0.039170	0.875431	0	0

5 rows × 26 columns

Finally, we see the effect of binning the numerical features.

```
#binning
est = preprocessing.KBinsDiscretizer(n_bins=10,
encode='ordinal', strategy='uniform')
est.fit(fords[['Year','Mileage','Price','Age']])
fords[['Year','Mileage','Price','Age']] = est.
transform(fords[['Year','Mileage','Price','Age']])
fords.head()
```

	Year	Mileage	Price	Age	Color_beige	Color_black	Color_blue
0	0.0	5.0	0.0	9.0	0	0	0
1	0.0	5.0	0.0	9.0	0	0	0
2	0.0	5.0	0.0	9.0	0	0	0
3	0.0	5.0	0.0	9.0	0	0	0
4	0.0	5.0	0.0	9.0	0	0	0

5 rows × 26 columns

And that is it!

Simple Linear Regression

In this chapter, we will begin working with regression analysis, as we will begin with simple linear regression. Although it is very simple compared to multiple regression and logistic regression, which we will explore in the next two chapters, the idea is the same.

We will start the chapter by defining a regression problem. Then, we will understand a very important concept in machine learning, which is supervised learning and how this is connected to predictor and response variables, which we mentioned earlier. After that, we will explore correlation analysis and see how it can be used as a measure for a linear relationship using the Statsmodels library in Python. With that, we will understand the coefficients of determination. Finally, we will explain the most-used optimization algorithms, gradient descent, and work on a hands-on project with Python step-by-step to implement everything that we learned through the chapter.

4.1. Defining a Regression problem

Imagine that you want to know if the income of a person has anything to do with the area of his/her house. To test this hypothesis, you asked many of your friends about both their income and their houses' areas. Or, you simply downloaded a dataset from the internet that fits your use case. Then, you will simply try to plot the data and see if there is a clear linear relationship. This plotting is done using a mathematical equation or a model, which can then be used to predict the income of a person by just knowing her/his house area.

This equation is a simple one, which is as follows:

$$y = mx + b$$

In this equation, we can find the output y by multiplying the input x by the slope m and adding this to the y-intercept b. The output is also called the response variable, as we are trying to evaluate or predict it. While the input can be called the predictor variables.

4.2. Supervised Learning

After we have defined the simplest regression problem, let us understand what is meant by supervised learning.

One goal for regression analysis is, as we have just seen, predict values—response variable. To achieve that, we need to learn how we can do so.

We start by having a dataset containing both the input and the output, and our goal is to find the slope b. Thus, when we have only the input data, we can multiply them by this slope, and we get the output with great accuracy. This is a **learning** process.

There are three main learning paradigms, which are supervised learning, unsupervised learning, and reinforcement learning.

The one that we will discuss is the first one—supervised learning.

In this paradigm, we have our dataset containing the input features—predictor variables—, and the output features—response variable. We try to predict the output from the input by training our machine learning model on the input and try to get as many correct predictions as possible.

Classification is one example of a machine learning algorithm where the goal is to classify objects. Regression is another example where we try to understand the relationships among variables.

4.3. Correlation Analysis

Now, let us understand what is meant by correlation analysis.

Correlation analysis is a statistical method to evaluate the strength of a relationship between two variables, which need to be numerical and continuous. It should be noted that **correlation does not imply causation**. This means that even if we find a positive or negative correlation between two variables, this tells us nothing about if one of them is the cause to the other or not. It clearly means that there is a relationship between these two variables, and that is it.

If there is a correlation, then this means that when we change one of them systematically, the other one also changes systematically. This change can be either in the same direction or in the opposite direction. Hence, the correlation can be positive or negative.

One of the most important coefficients used to evaluate the strength of the correlations is Pearson's coefficient. If we got +1, then this means that we have the strongest positive correlation possible, and if we got −1, then it means the opposite.

4.4. Correlation Analysis Using Statsmodels

Let us see how to use the Statsmodels library to perform correlation analysis.

We start by importing the needed libraries, of course.

```
import numpy as np
import statsmodels.api as sm
from scipy.stats import t
import random
```

Then, we load our dataset.

```
os.chdir('D:')
os.getcwd()
cars_df=pd.read_excel('cars.xls')
cars_df.head()
```

	Model	MPG	Cylinders	Displacement	Horsepower	Weight	Acceleration	Year	Origin
0	chevroletchevellemalibu	18.0	8	307.0	130	3504	12.0	70	US
1	buick skylark 320	15.0	8	350.0	165	3693	11.5	70	US
2	plymouth satellite	18.0	8	318.0	150	3436	11.0	70	US
3	amc rebel sst	16.0	8	304.0	150	3433	12.0	70	US
4	ford torino	17.0	8	302.0	140	3449	10.5	70	US

After that, we choose the MPG to be the input variable and the horsepower to be the output variable.

```
y=cars_df.MPG
X=cars_df.Horsepower
```

We make sure to split the dataset.

```
X_train,X_test,y_train,y_test=train_test_split(
pd.DataFrame(X),y,test_size=0.3,random_state=42)
```

Then, we add a constant column of ones, so we are having the same equation of the linear regression.

```
X_multi=sm.tools.tools.add_constant(X_train, prepend=True,
has_constant='skip')
```

After that, we perform the Ordinary Least Square (OLS) regression as below.

```
mod = sm.OLS(y_train, X_multi)
res = mod.fit()
print(res.summary())
```

```
                          OLS Regression Results
===============================================================================
Dep. Variable:                    MPG   R-squared:                      0.626
Model:                            OLS   Adj. R-squared:                 0.625
Method:                 Least Squares   F-statistic:                    455.7
Date:                Thu, 30 May 2019   Prob (F-statistic):          4.55e-60
Time:                        01:39:08   Log-Likelihood:               -823.78
No. Observations:                 274   AIC:                            1652.
Df Residuals:                     272   BIC:                            1659.
Df Model:                           1
Covariance Type:            nonrobust
===============================================================================
                 coef    std err          t      P>|t|      [0.025      0.975]
-------------------------------------------------------------------------------
const         41.0848      0.869     47.255      0.000      39.373      42.797
Horsepower    -0.1663      0.008    -21.348      0.000      -0.182      -0.151
===============================================================================
Omnibus:                       13.528   Durbin-Watson:                   2.150
Prob(Omnibus):                  0.001   Jarque-Bera (JB):               14.281
Skew:                           0.500   Prob(JB):                     0.000792
Kurtosis:                       3.499   Cond. No.                         327.
===============================================================================
```

4.5. Coefficient of Determination

To understand what the coefficient of determination—denoted R^2—and other important concepts are, we will need to go through the previous figure that contains OLS regression results.

First, we see that the dependent variable is MPG, as we have specified while preparing the data. Then, you will find some metadata such as the data, the time, the number of observations, and the type of covariance.

At the end of the results, we see some statistical tests that are done, such as Omnibus, Skew, Kurtosis, and Jarque-Bera. The details of these tests are out of the scope of this book and are rarely used anyway.

The most important things to look at from this figure are the R-squared and the adjusted R-square values.

R-squared, which is also called the coefficient of determination, can be formulated as follows:

$$R^2 = 1 - \frac{SS_{res}}{SS_{tot}}$$

Where,

$$SS_{res} = \sum_{i=1}^{n} r_i^2$$

$$SS_{tot} = \sum_{i=1}^{n} y_i^2$$

We know that r_i is the difference between the predicted value and the true value, also known as the residual. Therefore, we can say that R^2 is a measure of the reduction in the sum of squared values between the raw label values and the residuals. If $R^2 = 0$, then our model is useless and does not reduce the error. On the other hand, if $r_i = 0$, then $R^2 = 1$, which is our ultimate target.

Another variation of $R^2$is R_{adj}^2 which is the same except for the SS terms to be the variance of the residual and the variance of the true labels.

As we saw, both R² and adjusted R² are low, which indicates that the input variable cannot be used alone to predict the output variable correctly.

4.6. Optimization Algorithms

Going back to the simple linear regression analysis, we said that we want to **predict** the output by **training** a machine learning model on both the input and the output, so we can get the slope and use both the new input and the learned slope to predict the new output.

$$y = mx + b$$

So, our goal is to find m and b, which we will call the weights and the bias from now on. Let us take our example one step further and plot it.

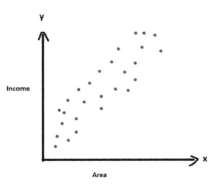

We can fit our model with different slopes, as we change b and m.

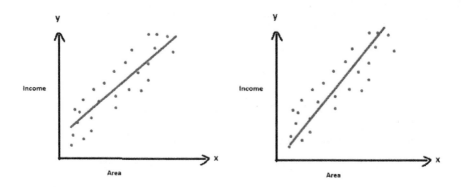

To stick to the machine learning notation, let's rename b to be w_0 and m to be w_1. So now, we can rewrite the equation this way:

$$y = w_0 + w_1 * x$$

As we can see, there are infinite values for the weights, and we cannot tell, until now, which set of weights gives the best performance.

There are two main methods to determine these weights. Both are based on minimizing the error. However, they differ in their approaches to do so, as the first method, as we will see, does this by getting a closed-form mathematical solution, while the second one is an iterative solution that tries to converge to the correct answer.

The first method is quite simple, as we say that the error is $\epsilon_i = y_i - \hat{y}_i$ where y_i is the true output, for example, / and $\hat{y}_i$ is the estimated output, for example, i. So, the error, which is also called the residual, is the difference between them. Our objective is to minimize the sum of the squared prediction errors. We use the square because we want to have all our errors to be positive values and eliminate any negative values. We could also minimize the sum of the absolute prediction errors, as this will also do the trick. However, using the squaring technique has some mathematical advantages over the absolute technique. Therefore, we will stick the sum of the squared error technique.

So, we can write this mathematically as follows:

$$E = \sum_{i=1}^{n}(y_i - \hat{y}_i)^2 = \sum_{i=1}^{n}(y_i - (w_0 + w_i x_i))^2$$

We can find *w* using some mathematical manipulation that we will not be concerned about right now, but it has a closed-form solution that is applied.

The second method is an iterative method called **gradient descent**. In this method, we have our cost function, which is the same as the sum of the squared errors. Our objective again is to find the weights that minimize the cost function as follows:

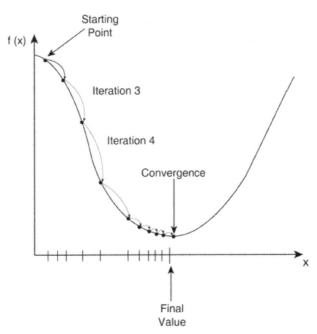

4.7. Gradient Descent

If you studied pre-calculus in high school, you would know that by saying minimize or maximize for a function, we mean getting the first derivative of this function and making this derivative equal to zero. The symbol that we will use for the derivative of the cost function is ∇J. The most common optimization algorithm used in machine learning for minimization is called gradient descent.

The intuition behind the gradient descent is very simple. You start by choosing random weights. Then you calculate the first derivative of the cost function. After that, you move in the opposite direction of this value, with multiplying this number by a factor called the learning rate. Finally, we update the weights and repeat until convergence.

$$w = w - \alpha \nabla J(w)$$

So, you might have two questions. The first one is what should be the value of the learning rate. The answer is that it depends on the convergence rate. So, if we have an error and far from the right answer, then we will want a bigger learning rate. However, once we start converging, this big learning rate will make it difficult for us to reach the minimum value as it may overshoot. Also, choosing a very small learning rate will make the model take too much time to converge, and it may also get stuck in a local minimum and do not reach the global minimum. Nonetheless, people tend to use the learning rate in the range of 10^{-2} – 10^{-5}. So, a good method to choose your learning rate is to start from 10^{-5} and increase it sharply if it gives you good results, then increase it carefully once you reach a critical value.

Note that the learning rate is not included in the trainable parameters of the model. Thus, we call it a *hyperparameter.*

The second question is why we take the negative of the gradient. The answer is that the derivative is the slope at this point, and the direction of that slope is in the opposite direction of the correct answer. Therefore, we use the negative sign in our calculation of the new weights.

It is also worth mentioning that it is preferred to use gradient-descent based learning than the closed-form solution when we have a large number of features because it becomes computationally expensive to find a closed-form solution.

4.8. Hands-On Project

Now, let us see how to perform simple linear regression using sklearn in Python.

We start with the libraries.

```
import pandas as pd
import os
import numpy as np
from sklearn.model_selection import train_test_split
from sklearn.linear_model import LinearRegression
import matplotlib.pyplot as plt
```

We load the data.

```
os.chdir('D:')
os.getcwd()
cars_df=pd.read_excel('cars.xls')
cars_df.head()
```

	Model	MPG	Cylinders	Displacement	Horsepower	Weight	Acceleration	Year	Origin
0	chevroletchevellemalibu	18.0	8	307.0	130	3504	12.0	70	US
1	buick skylark 320	15.0	8	350.0	165	3693	11.5	70	US
2	plymouth satellite	18.0	8	318.0	150	3436	11.0	70	US
3	amc rebel sst	16.0	8	304.0	150	3433	12.0	70	US
4	ford torino	17.0	8	302.0	140	3449	10.5	70	US

We then choose the input and output variables and split the data.

```
y=cars_df.MPG
X=cars_df.Horsepower
X_train,X_test,y_train,y_test=train_test_split(
pd.DataFrame(X),y,test_size=0.3,random_state=42)
```

Then, we fit the model using sklearn linear regression module.

```
regressor = LinearRegression()
regressor.fit(X_train, y_train)
```

After that, we test the model on the test data.

```
y_prediction = regressor.predict(X_test)
RMSE = sqrt(mean_squared_error(y_true = y_test, y_pred = y_
prediction))
print(RMSE)
4.955413560049774
```

Finally, let us plot the fitted slope to link everything together.

```
# add your actual vs. predicted points
plt.scatter(y_test, regressor.predict(X_test))
# add the line of perfect fit
straight_line = np.arange(0, 60)
plt.plot(straight_line, straight_line)
plt.title("Fitted Values")
plt.show()
```

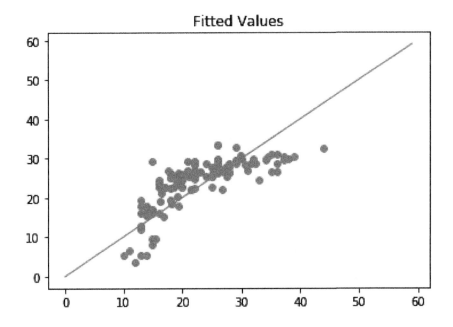

5

Multiple Linear Regression

After going through all the details about simple linear regression in the previous chapter, let us see in this chapter how we can expand this to multiple linear regression.

We will start the chapter by discussing how we can use multiple features to predict an output. Then, we will practice how we build a model using Statsmodels in Python. After that, we will see how to tweak the simple linear regression equation to be suitable for multiple linear regression. Following that, we will see also how we can scale up the correlation concept into a correlation matrix in multiple linear regression, along with the gradient descent concept.

Then, we explore feature scaling and unstandardized coefficients, which are key concepts to perform multiple regression correctly. After that, we will see how we can estimate the features' importance and the interaction effects in regression analysis. Following that, we will introduce polynomial regressions and reflect its concept on a very important machine learning concept, which is underfitting and overfitting.

Finally, we will connect everything by working on a hands-on project step-by-step.

5.1. Using Multiple features

Let us continue from where we left when we discussed the income estimation problem in the previous chapter. Back then, we assumed that we could estimate the income from just knowing the area of the house. But in fact, we need more information. This is because the more relevant information we have, the better we can estimate anything. So, for example, if we know the country that this person works in, the position that he/she has, the field, and any more relevant information, we can define a better regression model.

Each one of these variables is called a **feature.** Thus, we have multiple features, and hence multiple regression. However, if we have too many features, this might lead to worse estimation, as we will discuss by the end of this chapter when we introduce overfitting.

5.2. Multiple Linear Regression Using Statsmodels

Now, let us see how we can use Statsmodels to perform multiple linear regression. It is pretty like what we did in simple linear regression.

First, we import the needed libraries.

```
import pandas as pd
import os
import numpy as np
import statsmodels.api as sm
import matplotlib.pyplot as plt
```

Then, we import our dataset.

```
os.chdir('D:')
os.getcwd()
cars_df=pd.read_excel('cars.xls')
cars_df.head()
```

	Model	MPG	Cylinders	Displacement	Horsepower	Weight	Acceleration	Year	Origin
0	chevroletchevellemalibu	18.0	8	307.0	130	3504	12.0	70	US
1	buick skylark 320	15.0	8	350.0	165	3693	11.5	70	US
2	plymouth satellite	18.0	8	318.0	150	3436	11.0	70	US
3	amc rebel sst	16.0	8	304.0	150	3433	12.0	70	US
4	ford torino	17.0	8	302.0	140	3449	10.5	70	US

Then, we choose the MPG as our response variable and other variables as predictive variables.

```
y=cars_df.MPG
X=cars_df[['Cylinders', 'Displacement', 'Horsepower',
'Weight', 'Acceleration', 'Year', 'Origin']]
```

After that, we convert the categorical variables into dummy variables, as we discussed in chapter 3.

```
X=pd.get_dummies(X,drop_first=True)
```

Then, we split the dataset.

```
X_train,X_test,y_train,y_test=train_test_split(X,y,test_
size=0.3,random_state=4)
```

Then, we simply perform the regression analysis using Statsmodels the same way we did in simple linear regression.

```
X_multi=sm.tools.tools.add_constant(X_train,prepend=True,has_
constant='skip')
# OLS Regression
mod = sm.OLS(y_train, X_multi)
res = mod.fit()
print(res.summary())
```

```
                          OLS Regression Results
================================================================================
Dep. Variable:                  MPG   R-squared:                       0.826
Model:                          OLS   Adj. R-squared:                  0.821
Method:               Least Squares   F-statistic:                     157.8
Date:              Thu, 30 May 2019   Prob (F-statistic):           3.78e-96
Time:                      01:39:09   Log-Likelihood:                -718.66
No. Observations:               274   AIC:                             1455.
Df Residuals:                   265   BIC:                             1488.
Df Model:                         8
Covariance Type:            nonrobust
================================================================================
                  coef    std err          t      P>|t|      [0.025      0.975]
--------------------------------------------------------------------------------
const          -14.3960      5.861     -2.456      0.015     -25.935      -2.857
Cylinders       -0.3331      0.409     -0.814      0.416      -1.139       0.473
Displacement     0.0204      0.010      2.138      0.033       0.002       0.039
Horsepower      -0.0288      0.016     -1.747      0.082      -0.061       0.004
Weight          -0.0063      0.001     -8.003      0.000      -0.008      -0.005
Acceleration     0.0413      0.117      0.353      0.724      -0.189       0.271
Year             0.7782      0.066     11.766      0.000       0.648       0.908
Origin_Japan     0.0253      0.722      0.035      0.972      -1.397       1.447
Origin_US       -3.3369      0.727     -4.588      0.000      -4.769      -1.905
================================================================================
Omnibus:                     17.206   Durbin-Watson:                   2.012
Prob(Omnibus):                0.000   Jarque-Bera (JB):               20.888
Skew:                         0.510   Prob(JB):                     2.91e-05
Kurtosis:                     3.889   Cond. No.                     8.91e+04
================================================================================
```

We can see that R^2 and R^2_{adj} are 82.6 percent and 82.1 percent for multiple linear regression, which is much better than simple linear regression, where we got only 62.5% and 62.6 percent.

5.3. Multiple Linear Regression Equation

The simple linear regression equation was as follows:

$$y = w_0 + w_1 * x$$

Now, we have multiple weights, one for each feature. Also, x is composed of different features, so we need a subscript for it too. Therefore, the generalized linear regression formula is as follows:

$$y = \sum_{i=0}^{n} w_i x_i = w^T x$$

The *T* superscript that we use for w is called the transpose, and this equation is the same as the sum equation. But it is mainly used when we convert our variables into vectors and matrices. By converting them, we can avoid using loops, which takes too much time to finish if we have a large number of inputs. Using vectors is always preferable as computers are optimized to perform matrix multiplication more than loops. We call this paradigm *vectorization*.

Also, note that this equation is true for simple linear regression.

5.4. Gradient Descent and Correlation Matrix

For optimizing a multiple linear regression model, the same concepts apply. This means that we can use the same equation for gradient descent:

$$w = w - \alpha \nabla J(w)$$

But now, we have multiple equations equal to the number of features that we have in our model.

However, the new thing to know is that instead of correlating a single value, we now have a correlation matrix. This matrix is a fancy word for a table that shows the correlation coefficients between all the variables and each other.

The following figure is a practical example of what a correlation matrix looks like. Of course, the correlation along the diagonal is always 1 because the diagonal corresponds to the correlation between the variable and itself. We can also notice that the correlation between horsepower and displacement variables is 0.9, which means that we can predict the value of one of them given the other with high accuracy.

Also, note that we can use the correlation matrix to identify which variables are highly correlated so we can get rid of one of them if we want to reduce the size of our dataset. This can be crucial if we have an overfitting problem, as we will discuss shortly.

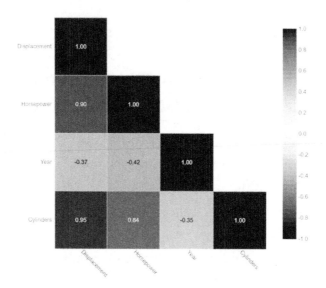

5.5. Feature Scaling and Unstandardized Coefficients

In simple linear regression, we had only one feature that we used to predict our output. However, in multiple linear regression, we have more than one feature. This led to a problem that we need to take care of, which is different scales for each variable.

In the following table, we are trying to predict the income from the house size, the number of bedrooms, and the number of floors.

House Size – m²	Bedrooms	Floors	Income
125	3	1	1500
200	3	2	1200
340	5	3	3000
115	4	1	1300

As we can see, the house sizes range from 115 m² to 340 m², while the number of bedrooms and floors from 1 to 5. This is a huge problem for the gradient descent algorithm because the range of the house sizes is huge, while the range of the other features is much smaller. This will lead the algorithm to find the best values of the weights for bedrooms and the floors quickly, while it will take much longer to do the same for the house size.

This will lead to a lot of confusion for the gradient descent as it updates all the weights and combines them to calculate the total loss, which will not reflect either the small features or the big features, but something in between.

To fix this problem, we need to perform feature scaling, which means changing the values of all features to be within the same range. This means that for any given feature x, we want every data point of it to be in the range of −1 and 1.

One way to do this is to find the maximum value of a given feature and divide all features by that value. For instance, from the table, we have 340m² as the maximum house size. So, if we divide every house size by 340, this will automatically scale the feature to be within a range of 0-1. We can do the same for the two other features.

Another way to tackle the problem is to perform *mean normalization*, which we discussed in chapter 3. This is done by getting the mean of every variable and subtracting the examples from it and dividing by the standard deviation of this variable. The formula for it is as follows:

$$X = \frac{X - \mu}{\sigma}$$

Another important concept is multiple linear regression is unstandardized coefficients. They are *raw* coefficients that result from regression analysis when it is performed on the dataset without standardization – which we covered thoroughly in chapter 3. While the standardized coefficients are normalized and unit-less, unstandardized coefficients have units and *real-life* scale.

The main advantage of not standardizing your dataset, and hence having unstandardized coefficients, is that they are intuitive to interpret and understand. This is because they represent the actual relation between raw data. Moreover, they can be used for comparisons if we applied feature scaling.

However, they are not preferred if we did not scale our features. This is because the output will be meaningless and uninterpretable.

5.6. Feature Importance Estimation and Interaction Effects

The interaction effect happens in regression analysis when the effect of the predictive variable on the response variable changes, based on the value of one or more of the other predictive variables. This is represented as a product of two or more predictive variables. The following equation is for multiple regression without an interaction.

$$y = w_0 + w_1 x_1 + w_2 x_2$$

And the following equation is when we consider interaction:

$$y = w_0 + w_1 x_1 + w_2 x_2 + w_3 x_2 x_3$$

In the last equation, w_3 is a regression coefficient, while $x_2 x_3$ is the interaction variable, which is also called a two-way interaction.

Now, to know if there is an interaction between two variables or not, we plot an interaction line graph. To do so, we follow these steps:

1. Plot the response variable on the y-axis and the predictive variable on the x-axis.

2. For each level of a potential interacting variable, plot the average score on the response variable separately.

3. Produce separate lines for each level of the interacting variable by connecting the average scores.

Then, to know if there is an interaction or not:

1. If the lines are parallel, this means there is no interaction.

2. If the lines are intersecting anywhere, this means that there is an interaction.

We will see in the hands-on project how we can do all this step-by-step.

Note also we can estimate the feature importance of the variables using different techniques. One technique is to fit the regression model using all predictive variables except one, then fit it again with all variables except another one. By keeping track of the loss, we can understand which variable is not that important in our estimation. Another technique is to look at the correlation matrix and the p-value in the Statsmodels summary results. If the correlation value between two variables is tending to 0 or/and the p-value is more than 0.05, then this means that we can remove this feature without hurting the prediction power of our model.

5.7. Polynomial Regression and Overfitting-Underfitting Tradeoff

Before we talk about what is meant by overfitting and underfitting, let us recall what we know so far about the main objective of regression analysis.

If you remember, the main objective is to recognize the pattern of the data, which can be measured by how well the algorithm performs on unseen data, not just the ones that the model was trained on.

This is called **generalization**, which is performing well on previously unseen input.

The problem in our discussion so far is that when we train our model, we calculate the training error. However, we can know more about the testing error (generalization error).

Therefore, we need to split our dataset into two sub-datasets, one for training and one for testing. For traditional machine learning algorithms like linear regression with small datasets (less than 50,000 instances), we usually split the dataset into 70 percent for training and 30 percent for testing. If the dataset is large (more than 50,000 instances), this we train on more than 70 percent and test on less than 30 percent.

Note that your model should not be exposed to the testing set throughout the training process.

You might ask now, are there any guarantees that this splitting operation will make that the two datasets have the same distribution?

This is hard to answer, but data science pioneers made all their algorithms based on the assumption that the data generation process is I.I.D., which means that the data are independent of each other and identically distributed.

So, what are the factors that determine how well the linear regression model is doing?

We can think of two main factors, which are making the training error small, and making the gap between the training error and testing error also small.

By defining these two factors, we can now introduce what is meant by **underfitting** and **overfitting**.

We say that the model is underfitting when the training error is large, as the model cannot capture the true complexity of the data.

We say that the model is overfitting when the gap between the training and testing errors is large, as the model is capturing even the noise among the data.

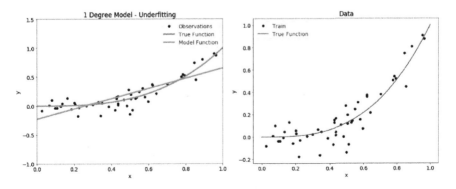

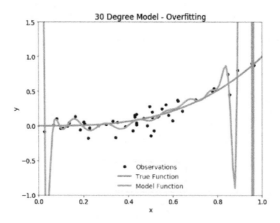

So, you might wonder, can we control this? The answer is yes, and it can be done by changing the model **capacity**. Capacity is a term that is used in many fields, but in the context of machine learning and regression analysis, it is a measure of how complex a relationship that the model can describe. We say that a model that represents quadratic function— **polynomial of the second degree**—has more capacity than the model that can represent a linear function.

You can relate the capacity to overfitting and underfitting by thinking of a dataset that follows a quadratic pattern. If your model is a linear function, then it will underfit the data no matter what you do. If your model is a cubic function— **polynomial of third-degree—**, then it will overfit the data.

Therefore, we can say that the model is performing well, if the capacity is appropriate for training data it is provided with, and the true complexity of the task it needs to perform. Given that knowledge, we can say with confidence that the model on the left is underfitting because it has low capacity, the model on the right is overfitting because it has a high capacity, and the model in the middle is just right because it has the appropriate capacity.

The solution of underfitting is straightforward:

1. Increasing the size of the dataset
2. Increasing the complexity of the model
3. Training the model for more time until it fits.

Overfitting solution is a bit trickier because it needs more carefulness:

1. Gather more data, of course. However, this solution is not always feasible.
2. Use cross-validation. So, let us stop here and know what is meant by cross-validation.

So far, we split our dataset into training and testing, and we said we train our model on the training set for the specified number of iterations, and after the training is finished, we test the model performance by using the test set. But what if we need to test our model after each iteration so we can know if the model is converging or diverging? This is where the validation set came to rescue. The validation dataset is simply another part of the dataset that is used for validating the performance of the model while it is still being trained. So, we split our dataset now into three datasets instead of two.

But the problem is, if the validation set is the same each time, we are back to square one again, which prevents us from using the testing set while training our model.

Therefore, to solve this problem, **K-fold cross-validation** was introduced. In this technique, the training dataset is split into k separate parts. The training process is repeated k times, with each time we randomly choose a subset that is held out for testing the model while the remaining subsets are used for training. The model overall error is the average error of all errors.

Leave-one-out cross-validation is a special type of k-fold cross-validation, where k is simply the number of instances in the dataset. So, each time we test only on one example and train on the rest. This method, of course, is not used because we cannot rely on one example. Another reason that it is not used is that it is computationally expensive as we will need to train our model numbers of time equal to the size of the dataset to get the overall error.

After understanding what is meant by cross-validation, we can now understand why it is used for preventing overfitting:

3. Because now, we can monitor our model and stop the training whenever the gap between the training error and validation error is increasing. This is called early stopping.

4. Regularization, which is penalizing the model if it is getting too complex for the problem at hand.

5.8. Hands-On Project

Now, let us see how to use Sklearn to perform regression analysis, and also understand interaction models.

We start, as always, by importing the libraries.

```
import pandas as pd
import os
import numpy as np
from sklearn.model_selection import train_test_split
from sklearn.linear_model import LinearRegression
from math import sqrt
from sklearn.metrics import mean_squared_error
import statsmodels.api as sm
import matplotlib.pyplot as plt
from sklearn.preprocessing import MinMaxScaler
import scipy as sp
import seaborn as sns
import statsmodels.formula.api as smf
```

Then we load the dataset.

```
os.chdir('D:')
os.getcwd()
cars_df=pd.read_excel('cars.xls')
cars_df.head()
```

	Model	MPG	Cylinders	Displacement	Horsepower	Weight	Acceleration	Year	Origin
0	chevroletchevellemalibu	18.0	8	307.0	130	3504	12.0	70	US
1	buick skylark 320	15.0	8	350.0	165	3693	11.5	70	US
2	plymouth satellite	18.0	8	318.0	150	3436	11.0	70	US
3	amc rebel sst	16.0	8	304.0	150	3433	12.0	70	US
4	ford torino	17.0	8	302.0	140	3449	10.5	70	US

After that, we split the data.

```
y=cars_df.MPG
X=cars_df[['Cylinders', 'Displacement', 'Horsepower',
'Weight', 'Acceleration', 'Year', 'Origin']]
```

As before, we create a dummy variable for the categorical feature.

```
X=pd.get_dummies(X,drop_first=True)
```

Then, we split the data into train and test.

```
X_train,X_test,y_train,y_test=train_test_split(X,y,
test_size=0.3,random_state=4)
```

Then, we perform feature scaling.

```
scaler=MinMaxScaler()
X_train_sc=pd.DataFrame(scaler.fit_transform(X_train),
columns=X_train.columns)
X_test_sc=pd.DataFrame(scaler.transform(X_test),
columns=X_test.columns)
```

Finally, we train linear regression model and test it on our test set.

```
regressor = LinearRegression()
regressor.fit(X_train_sc, y_train)
```

```
y_prediction = regressor.predict(X_test_sc)
RMSE = sqrt(mean_squared_error(y_true = y_test, y_pred = y_
prediction))
print(RMSE)
3.216235254988254
```

Now, let us understand the interaction models more. Suppose that your target variable is the *MPG*, and we want to know how the *Weight* variable affects the relationship between the *Cylinder's* variable and the *MPG* variable. The first step is to plot the Miles per gallon on the y-axis and the Vehicle weight on the x-axis.

```
sns.lmplot(x='Weight', y='MPG', hue='Cylinders', data=cars_df,
fit_reg=False, palette='viridis', size=5, aspect=2.5)
plt.ylabel("Miles per Gallon")
plt.xlabel("Vehicle Weight");
```

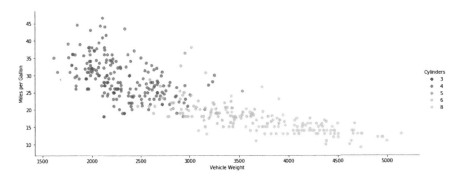

Now, let us build a regression model which has the following equation:

$$MPG = w_0 + w_1 Weight + w_2 Cylinders$$

```
model = smf.ols(formula='MPG ~ Weight + Cylinders', data=cars_
df).fit()
summary = model.summary()
summary.tables[1]
```

	coef	std err	t	P>|t|	[0.025	0.975]
Intercept	46.2923	0.794	58.305	0.000	44.731	47.853
Weight	-0.0063	0.001	-10.922	0.000	-0.007	-0.005
Cylinders	-0.7214	0.289	-2.493	0.013	-1.290	-0.152

From the coefficient column, we have the values of the weights, and we can write the equation again as follows:

$$MPG = 46.2923 - 0.0063 Weight - 0.7214 Cylinders$$

These coefficients can be interpreted as follows:

- For every unit increase in the weight variable, mpg decreases by 0.0063, assuming the cylinder's variable is constant.

- For every unit increase in the cylinder's variable, mpg decreases by 0.7214, assuming the weight variable is constant.

We can also notice that all p-values (the fourth column) are significant. We say that the p-value is significant if it is less than 0.05.

For any variable in the regression model, we must select one of two hypotheses:

1. Null hypothesis: The coefficient for this variable is zero.

2. Alternative hypothesis: The coefficient for this variable is not zero.

If the p-value for a variable is significant—less than 0.05—then we reject the null hypothesis. Therefore, we reject the null hypothesis for both variables.

Now, let us model the interaction between the weight variable and the cylinder's variable.

We can do so using two ways. The first way is as follows.

```
model_interaction = smf.ols(formula='MPG ~ Weight + Cylinders
+ Weight:Cylinders', data=cars_df).fit()
summary = model_interaction.summary()
summary.tables[1]
```

	coef	std err	t	P>|t|	[0.025	0.975]
Intercept	65.3865	3.733	17.514	0.000	58.046	72.727
Weight	-0.0128	0.001	-9.418	0.000	-0.016	-0.010
Cylinders	-4.2098	0.724	-5.816	0.000	-5.633	-2.787
Weight:Cylinders	0.0011	0.000	5.226	0.000	0.001	0.002

We see that the equation now becomes:

$$MPG = 65.3865 - 0.0128Weight - 4.2098Cylinders + 0.0011WeightCylinders$$

You can also notice that the p-value for the interaction variable is significant, confirming an interaction between the two variables.

The second way to model the interaction is by adding another variable, which is the multiplication of the two variables.

```
cars_df['wt_cyl'] = cars_df.Weight * cars_df.Cylinders

model_multiply = smf.ols(formula='MPG ~ Weight + Cylinders +
wt_cyl', data=cars_df).fit()
summary = model_multiply.summary()
summary.tables[1]
```

	coef	std err	t	P>|t|	[0.025	0.975]
Intercept	65.3865	3.733	17.514	0.000	58.046	72.727
Weight	-0.0128	0.001	-9.418	0.000	-0.016	-0.010
Cylinders	-4.2098	0.724	-5.816	0.000	-5.633	-2.787
Weight:Cylinders	0.0011	0.000	5.226	0.000	0.001	0.002

Now, let us plot the interaction graph using the steps that we explained earlier.

```
cars_df['cyl_med'] = cars_df.Cylinders>cars_df.Cylinders.
median()
cars_df['cyl_med'] = np.where(cars_df.cyl_med == False, "Below
Median", "Above Median")
sns.lmplot(x='Weight', y='MPG', hue='cyl_med', data=cars_df,
ci=None, size=5, aspect=2.5);
```

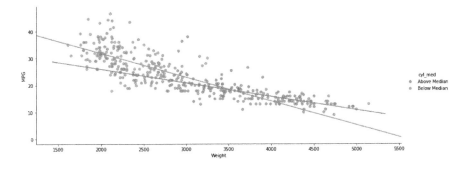

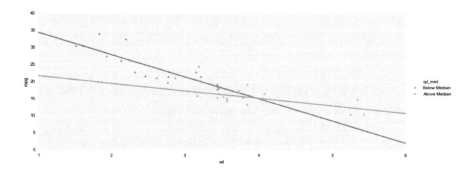

We can deduce from this graph that when the cylinder value is small—below the median—the relationship between *MPG* and *Weight* is strongly negative. While on the other side, when the cylinder value is big—above-median—the relationship between *MPG* and *Weight* is weaker.

Finally, we can deduce that the larger the differences in slopes, the larger the interaction effect.

6

Logistic Regression

So far, we have discussed only regression problems, such as estimating prices, ages, or anything. However, in this chapter, we will focus on classification problems, such as classifying if someone has a disease or not by looking at his/her medical record.

While there are many classification algorithms, we will focus on only one of them, which is logistic regression. The reason is that logistic regression is very similar to linear regression, so there are no entirely new concepts, but rather a modification to the algorithm.

We will start by defining a classification problem. Then, we will see how we can evaluate the performance of our classifier. After that, we will understand the intuition behind logistic regression, and how to use gradient descent on it. Following that, we will discuss the pros and cons of using logistic regression. Finally, we will connect everything by working on a hands-on project step-by-step.

6.1. Defining a Classification Problem

The main difference between regression and classification is that in regression, we try to estimate a value in continuous space with no restriction, while in classification, our goal is to estimate also a value but within a discrete space with limited value. For example, in house price estimation, the house price can be any value, while in dog breed classification, we try to predict to which breed the current image of a dog belongs, so we know beforehand that it has to be one of 100 possible values if we assume that there are only 100 dog breeds in the world.

6.2. Evaluating the Classifier Performance

Now, a very important question is how we can tell if the classifier is performing well or not? And what is even the definition of "good" in this context?

Luckily, we have a few metrics that we can use to evaluate classifier performance:

1. **Accuracy:** Where we report the number of predicted outputs that match the true outputs.

2. **Confusion Matrix:** We can see the confusion matrix in the following figure.

		True condition	
	Total population	Condition positive	Condition negative
Predicted condition	Predicted condition positive	**True positive**	**False positive,** Type I error
	Predicted condition negative	**False negative,** Type II error	**True negative**

From the confusion matrix, we can get the accuracy which is,

$$Accuracy = \frac{TP + TN}{P + N}$$

Also, we can get another two metrics called the precision and the recall:

$$Precision = Positive\ Predictive\ Value = \frac{TP}{TP + FP}$$

$$Recall = Sensitivity = True\ Positive\ Rate = \frac{TN}{TP + FN}$$

And, we can also get a combination of the precision and the recall called the F-score as follows:

$$F = \frac{2}{\frac{1}{Recall} + \frac{1}{Precision}}$$

So, why do we not just get the accuracy? Why do we need precision and recall?

To answer these questions, let us look at two different classification problems and see if the accuracy is the best evaluation metric to use.

Suppose that you have a spam vs. non-spam classification problem where you classify emails to be either spam or ham. So, we have two different kinds of errors, which are the false positives and the false negatives. The false positives occur when we misclassify a ham email as a spam email, and the false negatives occur when we misclassify a spam email as a ham email. Which of these two errors are more critical? I think you agree with me that not putting an important email into the spam folder is more crucial than getting annoyed with a spam email into your main email folder. Of course, both are considered types of errors. But in our problem, we care more about having the minimum number of false positives. Thus, we use **precision** as our metric when evaluating the model.

For the second problem, suppose we have a cancer detection problem, wherewith we classify the patients to either have cancer or not. Again, we have two types of errors, which are predicting that a healthy patient has cancer and predicting that a sick patient does not have cancer. In contrast to the first example, here, we care more about the false negatives, because of the nature of the problem itself. We really do not want a cancer patient to be classified as healthy, but we can accept that some of our healthy patients are misclassified because then they will do more tests, and they will find themselves healthy afterward. Thus, we use **recall** as our evaluation metric.

If we want a **harmonic mean** between accuracy and recall, then we use the **F-score.**

3. **ROC curve:** Short for Receiver Operating Characteristic. ROC curve is just a plot of the False Positive Rate against the True Positive Rate. It is used mainly to select the optimum model which should have an area under the curve—AUC—equal to or near 1. This is because the True Positive Rate should be equal to or near 1, while the False Positive Rate should be equal to or near 0. Moreover, a random classifier is found to have an AUC of 0.5.

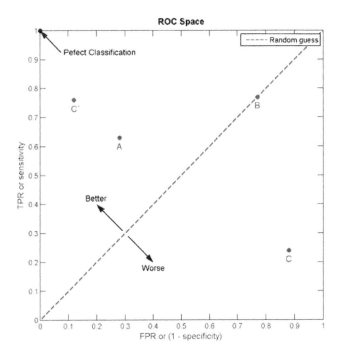

6.3. Logistic Regression Intuition

In linear regression, we saw how we could perform regression analysis using the linear regression equation with the gradient descent to update the weights. Now, we will do something very similar but for classification purposes.

To simplify the classification problem and focus only on the algorithm of logistic regression, we will assume, for now, that have only two classes. So, we can treat our problem as a binary classification problem. For example, we would predict if a student will be accepted in a specific university or not.

Therefore, we can formalize our output as a probability from [0,1], and if it is above a certain threshold, 0.5 for example, then this student will get accepted, and if it is less than the threshold, then he will get rejected.

However, the equation that we used for linear regression is not limited by this constraint. So, we use a *logistic* function to transform our output to be in the range [0,1] so we can treat it as a probability. The most famous and currently used logistic function is the *sigmoid* which has the following equation:

$$y(z) = \frac{1}{1 + e^{-z}}$$

Where z is the linear equation that we used in linear regression:

$$z = \sum_{i=0}^{n} w_i x_i = w^T x$$

To understand how the sigmoid function squashes our input into [0,1], we can plot it using Python, and we would get the following curve.

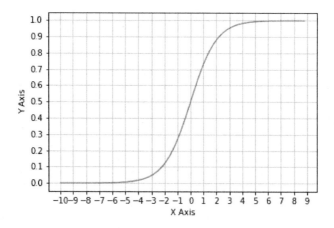

We can generate this plot by simply writing the sigmoid as a Python function and then call this function with different values of input.

As you can see, the output—Y-axis—can only take values in the range [0,1], and it reaches zero at negative infinity and reaches one at positive infinity. We can also see that the output is 0.5 when the input is zero. We can alter that by scaling the sigmoid function or changing the bias.

6.4. Logistic Regression Gradient Descent

Moving to the loss function, we cannot use the same mean square error loss that we used for linear regression, as the numbers are all between 0 and 1 so the results will be significant. Thus, we need a loss function that is sensitive to small changes. To do so, we use the *negative log-likelihood* loss function, which is defined as follows:

$$J(w) = -\sum_i \left(y^i \log \left(h_w(x^i) \right) + \left(1 - y^i \right) \log \left(1 - h_w(x^i) \right) \right)$$

There is no closed-form solution to calculate the weights as in linear regression. Therefore, the only possible way to estimate the weights is to use an iterative solution such as gradient descent.

The mathematics behind the final output is complex, so the only thing that you need to know is that gradient descent and other iterative optimization algorithms are **the only way** to update the weights in logistics regression and hence classify the output correctly.

One of the most frequent problems that many people face when they try to implement and run logistic regression is overfitting. So, we use a technique called regularization to address this problem.

Regularization is a fancy word for the penalty as we penalize the model if it is getting more complex. We can understand this better by looking at how we update the weights when we introduce the regularization term.

$$w = w - \alpha \frac{\partial J(w)}{\partial x} - \lambda \alpha w$$

We say that α is the learning rate and λ is the penalization term. So, we see that the regularization term is added as a second term in the loss function. The purpose of this regularization term is to push the parameters toward smaller numbers, and thus, the model does not become more complex, and hence, it does not overfit.

There are many different methods to implement the regularization term. However, the two most used ways are the **Lasso method**, also called "L1," and the **Ridge method**, which is also called "L2."

The main difference between the two methods is that the Lasso method tries to push all the parameters toward zero, while the Ridge method tries to push all the parameters toward very small numbers but not equal to zero. Both methods are used, and you need to experiment with both to know which one works best for each specific case.

6.5. Logistic Regression Pros and Cons

Now, let us summarize the pros and cons of logistic regression.

- **Pros:**
  a. Very easy to understand and interpret.
  b. Very fast to train and to predict.
  c. Works well with sparse data if we use regularization.

- **Cons:**

    a. Requires the data to be probably pre-processed and scaled.

    b. It does not work very well, compared to more complex algorithms, especially if the data is complex by nature.

6.6. Hands-On Project

Now, let us see how to use Sklearn to perform logistic regression analysis.

We start, as always, by importing the libraries.

```
from sklearn.linear_model import LogisticRegression
from sklearn.model_selection import train_test_split
from sklearn.preprocessing import StandardScaler,MinMaxScaler
from sklearn import metrics
from sklearn.metrics import accuracy_score
import pandas as pd
import numpy as np
import os
import matplotlib.pyplot as plt
import seaborn as sns
```

Then, we load the dataset.

```
os.chdir('D:')
os.getcwd()
credit=pd.read_csv('german_credit.csv')
print(credit.info())
<class 'pandas.core.frame.DataFrame'>
RangeIndex: 1000 entries, 0 to 999
Data columns (total 22 columns):
Customer_ID                 1000 non-null int64
checking_account_status     1000 non-null object
loan_duration_mo            1000 non-null int64
credit_history              1000 non-null object
purpose                     1000 non-null object
loan_amount                 1000 non-null int64
savings_account_balance     1000 non-null object
time_employed_yrs           1000 non-null object
payment_pcnt_income         1000 non-null int64
gender_status               1000 non-null object
other_signators             1000 non-null object
time_in_residence           1000 non-null int64
property                    1000 non-null object
age_yrs                     1000 non-null int64
other_credit_outstanding    1000 non-null object
home_ownership              1000 non-null object
number_loans                1000 non-null int64
job_category                1000 non-null object
dependents                  1000 non-null int64
telephone                   1000 non-null object
foreign_worker              1000 non-null object
bad_credit                  1000 non-null int64
dtypes: int64(9),object(13)
```

Then, we choose the bad credit variable to be the output variable that we want to predict and classify.

```
Y=credit['bad_credit']
```

Then, we create a dummy variable for the credit categorical variable.

```
X=pd.get_dummies(credit)
```

After that, we split the dataset, scale it, and train it.

```
X_train,X_test,Y_train,Y_test=train_test_split(X,
Y,test_size=0.3,random_state=42)
scaler=MinMaxScaler()
X_train=pd.DataFrame(scaler.fit_transform(X_train),
columns=X_train.columns)
X_test=pd.DataFrame(scaler.transform(X_test),
columns=X_test.columns)
logreg=LogisticRegression()
mod1=logreg.fit(X_train,Y_train)
```

Now, let us test our model.

```
pred1=logreg.predict(X_test)
accuracy_score(y_true=Y_test, y_pred=pred1)
0.77
```

Let us also plot the weight for each feature to see how important it is.

```
plt.figure(figsize=(15,10))
plt.bar(X_train.columns.tolist(),logreg.coef_[0])
plt.xticks(rotation=90,size=10)
plt.show()
```

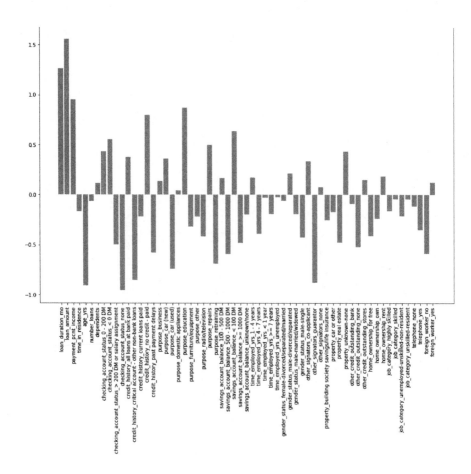

Now, let us see what the results would be with either L1 or L2 regularization.

```
logreg1=LogisticRegression(penalty='l1',C=1)
mod2=logreg1.fit(X_train,Y_train)
pred2=logreg1.predict(X_test)
accuracy_score(y_true=Y_test, y_pred=pred2)
0.7566666666666667
```

```
logreg2=LogisticRegression(penalty='l2',C=0.01)
mod3=logreg2.fit(X_train,Y_train)
pred3=logreg2.predict(X_test)
accuracy_score(y_true=Y_test, y_pred=pred3)
0.7
```

As we can see, the results became worse, which means that we need more data as the model is underfitting and not overfitting.